THE BREAD MACHINE
COOKBOOK

200 recipes to make all types of bread with any machine and bake like your favorite bakery, whether you are a beginner or a pro!

Nancy Hollywood

Contents

Introduction

Making bread is a great activity. It has a potential calming effect and, most importantly, provides the deep inner satisfaction of serving warm homemade bread to your family and friends.

To make incredible homemade bread, you need the right recipe, set your machine, and gather the right ingredients. The device will take care of the entire process: it will knead, rise and bake. All you'll have left to do will be to wait for the timer to ding and enjoy warm, soft bread.

You can make bread with herbs, cheese, meat or vegetables. You can make gluten-free or keto bread and even use your bread machine to make desserts: the options are endless!

This book is meant to be your new ally: you can finally say goodbye to bread filled with artificial preservatives and food coloring and find out what freshness really tastes like.

It doesn't matter which bread machine you have, the recipes included in this book can be made with any device. Some new generation machines have bonus features and have faster baking cycles, but don't worry, you will learn your machine's times and power easily.

Before you pick up the first recipe to try, read the instructions below to have a fuller picture of how most machines usually work:

Most machines have an LCD screen with a control panel on the top to tell the machine what to do. There are specific recipes for each type of cycle.

These cycles may use two, 1.5, 1, 1, or 0.5-pound loaves. The flour amount needed varies greatly depending on the specific recipe used.

The first cycle starts by mixing flours, water, butter, sugar, and yeast to get the yeast to activate. Yeast is used for all dough recipes. It begins activating when you include a packet of yeast with the ingredients. This will help the yeast to start to ferment the ingredients into a dough.

The next step is to add slowly whatever ingredients are needed to the flour for the recipe. In the case of white bread, ingredients are milk, butter, salt, and sugar. Begin the first cycle by adding the ingredients to the machine. If you add ingredients in this order, the machine will produce bread.

After adding all of the ingredients, close the lid. Turn on the machine to begin the first cycle.

If there is not enough water in the water container, use bottled water. Most machines have a separate water sprayer, but if the water sprayer is not working, use water from the water container. The water that comes out of the sprayer is the same as the water in the box. You will have no problems with the machine not producing bread if you do not use the water sprayer. The device will keep reading the ingredients throughout the entire process.

The first stage of the cycle makes the bread rise. This is a critical stage of the process. This phase of the cycle usually takes longer than other cycles. The yeast uses this time to ferment your ingredients.

The second stage, which is only a few minutes long, is when the liquid ingredients are added into the bread mix. The ingredients consist of eggs, butter, vegetable oil, or water. The butter that is added by this stage creates additional steam to help the bread rise as it bakes.
formula: 1 egg, 1 tablespoon vinegar, and 1.5 ounces water.

The final stage is when the bread can be removed from the machine to finish baking.

To prevent your bread from falling apart, it is necessary to bake the bread inside the machine before removing it. If you try to remove your bread from the machine before it is completely cooled, it is more likely that it will break apart. Many bread makers are equipped with a heating unit that bakes the bread after the cycle has ended. This heating unit is activated when the oven door is opened.

Dedication

To my daughters Rose and Emily who pushed me to start this book and are my best fans.
I love you with all my heart.

Gluten-free
ANAAMA BREAD

Servings: **1 loaf (12 slices)**

Preparation time: **2 hours**

Cook time: **60 minutes**

Ingredients

- One package (1/4 oz.) of active dry yeast
- 1 tbsp. sugar
- 1 cup warm water (110°-115°)
- Two large eggs
- 3 tbsps. canola oil
- 1 tbsp. molasses
- 1 tsp. white vinegar
- 1-1/2 cups gluten-

Directions

1. Grease 8x4-in. Loaf pan. Sprinkle using gluten-free flour put aside.

2. Melt sugar and yeast in warm water. Mix the vinegar, molasses, oil and eggs in a stand mixer's bowl with a paddle attachment. Then Add Whisk, xanthan gum, cornmeal and flour.

3. Beat for one minute on low speed beat for two minutes on medium speed. The dough will be softer compared to yeast bread dough that has

4. gluten. Put in prepped pan use a wet spatula to smooth top. Rise with cover for 40 minutes until the dough reaches the pan's lid in a warm

free all-purpose baking flour

- 3/4 cup cornmeal
- 1-1/2 tsp. xanthan gum
- 1/2 tsp. salt

place.

5. Bake for 20 minutes at 375°, then loosely cover using foil. Bake till golden brown for 10-15 minutes more

6. turn the oven off. In an oven, leave bread for 15 minutes with the door ajar. Transfer from pan onto a wire rack. Allow cooling.

Nutritional Information:

- Calories: 136 calories
- Total Carbohydrate: 21 g
- Cholesterol: 35 mg
- Total Fat: 5 g
- Fibre: 3 g
- Protein: 4 g
- Sodium: 115 mg

SANDWICH BREAD

Servings: **1 loaf (16 slices).**

Preparation time: **2 hours**
Cook time: **1 Hour**

Ingredients

- 1 tbsp. active dry yeast
- 2 tbsps. sugar
- 1 cup warm fat-free milk (110° to 115°)
- Two eggs
- 3 tbsps. canola oil
- 1 tsp. cider vinegar
- 2-1/2 cups gluten-free all-purpose baking flour
- 2-1/2 tsp. xanthan

Directions

1. Oil a loaf pan, 9x5 inches in size, and dust with gluten-free flour reserve.

2. In warm milk, melt sugar and yeast in a small bowl—mix yeast mixture, vinegar, oil, and eggs in a stand with a paddle. Slowly whip in salt, gelatin, xanthan gum and flour. Whip for a minute on low speed. Whip for 2 minutes on moderate. The dough will become softer compared to the yeast bread dough that has gluten. Turn onto the prepped pan. Using a wet spatula, smoothen the surface. Put a cover and rise in a warm area for 25 minutes until dough extends to the pan top.

3. Bake for 20 minutes at 375° loosely cover with foil. Bake till golden brown for 10 to 15

gum
- 1 tsp. unflavored gelatin
- 1/2 tsp. salt

minutes more. Take out from pan onto a wire rack to let cool.

Nutrition Information

- Calories: 110 calories
- Total Carbohydrate: 17 g
- Cholesterol: 27 mg
- Total Fat: 4 g
- Fiber: 2 g
- Protein: 4 g
- Sodium: 95 mg

ROSEMARY BREAD

Servings: 8 pcs

Preparation time: 2 hours

Cook time: 1 Hour

Ingredients

- 300ml (1 ¼ cups) warm water
- 60ml (¼ cup) olive oil
- Two egg whites
- One tablespoon apple cider vinegar
- ½ teaspoon baking powder
- Two teaspoons dry active yeast
- Two tablespoons granulated sugar
- ½ teaspoon Italian seasoning

Directions

1. According to your bread machine manufacturer, place all the ingredients into the bread machine's greased pan.

2. Select basic cycle / standard cycle/bake / quick bread / white bread setting
then choose crust color either medium or Light and press start to bake bread.

3. In the last kneading cycle, check the dough
it should be wet but thick, not like traditional bread dough. If the dough is too wet, put more flour, one tablespoon at a time, or until dough slightly firm.

4. When the cycle is finished, and the baker machine turns off, remove baked bread from pan and cool on wire rack.

- ¼ teaspoon ground black pepper
- 1¼ teaspoon dried rosemary
- 200g (2 cups) gluten-free almond flour / or any other gluten-free flour, levelled
- 100g (1 cup) Tapioca/potato starch, levelled
- Two teaspoons Xanthan Gum
- One teaspoon salt

Nutrition Information

- Calories: 150 Calories
- Total fat: 3 g
- Cholesterol: 5 mg
- Sodium: 290 mg
- Carbohydrates: 24 g
- Fibre: 1 g
- Protein: 6 g

FLAX AND SUNFLOWER SEEDS BREAD

Servings: 8 pcs

Preparation time: 2 hours

Cook time: : 1 Hour

Ingredients

- 300ml (1 ¼ cups) warm water
- 60ml (¼ cup) olive oil
- Two egg whites
- One tablespoon apple cider vinegar
- ½ teaspoon baking powder
- 7g (2 teaspoons) dry

Directions

1. According to your bread machine manufacturer, place all the ingredients into the bread machine's greased pan except sunflower seeds.

2. Select basic cycle / standard cycle/bake / quick bread / white bread setting
then select crust colour either medium or light and press start.

3. In the last kneading cycle, check the dough
it should be wet but thick, not like traditional bread

active yeast

- Two tablespoons granulated sugar
- 200g (2 cups) gluten-free almond flour / or any other gluten-free flour, levelled
- 100g (1 cup) Tapioca/potato starch, levelled
- Two teaspoons Xanthan Gum
- One teaspoon salt
- 55g (½ cup) flax seeds
- 55g (½ cup) sunflower seeds

dough. If the dough is too wet, put more flour, one tablespoon at a time, or until dough slightly firm.

4. Add sunflower seeds 5 minutes before the kneading cycle ends.

5. When the cycle is finished and the machine turns off, remove baked bread from pan and cool on wire rack.

Nutrition Information

- Calories: 90 Calories
- Total fat: 2g
- Cholesterol: 5 mg
- Sodium: 180 mg
- Carbohydrates: 18 g
- Fibre: 2 g
- Protein: 4 g

ITALIAN PARMESAN CHEESE BREAD

Servings: 6 pcs.

Preparation time: 2 hours

Cook time: : 1 Hour

Ingredients

- 300ml (1 ¼ cups) warm water
- 60ml (¼ cup) olive oil
- Two egg whites
- One tablespoon apple cider vinegar
- ½ teaspoon baking powder
- 7g (2 teaspoons) dry active yeast

Directions

1. According to your bread machine manufacturer, place all the ingredients into the bread machine's greased pan and select a basic cycle / standard cycle/bake / quick bread / white bread setting. Then choose crust colour, either medium or light and press start to bake bread.

2. In the last kneading cycle, check the dough it should be wet but thick, not like traditional bread dough. If the dough is too wet, put more flour, one tablespoon at a time, or until dough slightly firm.

3. When the cycle is finished and the machine turns off, remove baked bread from pan and cool on wire rack.

- Two tablespoons granulated sugar
- 200g (2 cups) gluten-free almond flour / or any other gluten-free flour, levelled
- 100g (1 cup) Tapioca/potato starch, levelled
- Two teaspoons Xanthan Gum
- 28g (¼ cup) grated Parmesan cheese
- One teaspoon salt
- One teaspoon Italian seasoning
- One teaspoon garlic powder

Nutrition Information

- Calories: 90 Calories
- Total fat: 2 g
- Cholesterol: 2 mg
- Sodium: 48 mg
- Carbohydrates: 15g
- Fibre: 1 g
- Protein: 2 g

CHEESE & HERB BREAD

Servings: **1 loaf (12 slices)**

Preparation time: **2 hours**

Cook time: : **1 Hour**

Ingredients

- 300ml (1 ¼ cups) warm water
- 60ml (¼ cup) olive oil
- Two egg whites
- One tablespoon apple cider vinegar
- ½ teaspoon baking powder
- 7g (2 teaspoons) dry active yeast

Directions

1. According to your bread machine manufacturer, place all the ingredients into the bread machine's greased pan, and select a basic cycle / standard cycle/bake / quick bread / white bread setting. Then choose crust colour, either medium or light, and press start to bake bread.

2. In the last kneading cycle, check the dough it should be wet but thick, not like traditional bread dough. If the dough is too wet, put more flour, one tablespoon at a time, or until dough slightly firm.

3. When the cycle is finished and the machine turns off,

- Two tablespoons granulated sugar
- 200g (2 cups) gluten-free almond flour / or any other gluten-free flour, levelled
- 100g (1 cup) Tapioca/potato starch, levelled
- Two teaspoons Xanthan Gum
- One teaspoon salt
- Two tablespoons grated Parmesan cheese
- One teaspoon dried marjoram
- ¾ teaspoon dried basil
- ¾ teaspoon dried oregano

remove baked bread from pan and cool on wire rack.

Nutrition Information

- Calories: 150 Calories
- Total fat: 3 g
- Cholesterol: 5 mg
- Sodium: 415 mg
- Carbohydrates: 9 g
- Fibre: 1 g
- Protein: 4 g

CINNAMON RAISIN BREAD

Servings: 1 loaf (12 slices)

Preparation time: 2 hours

Cook time: : 1 Hour

Ingredients

- 300ml (1 ¼ cups) warm water
- 60ml (¼ cup) olive oil
- Two tablespoons honey
- Two egg whites
- One tablespoon apple cider vinegar
- ½ teaspoon baking powder
- 7g (2 teaspoons) dry active yeast

Directions

1. According to your bread machine manufacturer, place all the ingredients into the bread machine's greased pan except raisins.

2. Select basic cycle / standard cycle/bake / quick bread / sweet bread setting
then choose crust colour either medium or Light and press start to bake bread.

3. In the last kneading cycle, check the dough
it should be wet but thick, not like traditional bread dough. If the dough is too wet, put more flour, one tablespoon at a time, or until dough slightly firm.

4. Add raisins 5 minutes before the kneading cycle ends.

- Two tablespoons granulated sugar
- 200g (2 cups) gluten-free almond flour / or any other gluten-free flour, levelled
- 100g (1 cup) Tapioca/potato starch, levelled
- Two teaspoons Xanthan Gum
- One teaspoon salt
- One teaspoon ground cinnamon
- 150g (1 cup) raisins

5. When the cycle is finished and the machine turns off, remove baked bread from pan and cool on wire rack.

Nutrition Information

- Calorie: 89 Calories
- Fat: 1 g
- Cholesterol: 2 mg
- Sodium: 10 mg
- Carbohydrates: 12 g

Chapter 1: Variety of flours

ALMOND FLOUR BREAD

Servings: 10 pcs

Preparation time: 10 minutes

Cook time: : 10 minutes

Ingredients

- Four egg whites
- Two egg yolks
- 2 cups almond flour
- 1/4 cup butter, melted
- 2 tbsp psyllium husk powder

Directions

1. Use a mixing bowl to combine all of the dry ingredients except for the yeast.
2. In the bread machine pan, add all the wet ingredients.
3. Add all of your dry ingredients from the small mixing bowl to the bread machine pan.
4. Set the machine to the basic setting.
5. When the bread is finished, remove it to the machine pan

- 1 1/2 tbsp baking powder
- 1/2 tsp xanthan gum
- Salt
- 1/2 cup + 2 tbsp warm water
- 2 1/4 tsp yeast

from the bread machine.

6. Let cool slightly before transferring to a cooling rack.

7. It can be stored for four days on the counter and three months in the freezer.

Nutrition Information

- Calories: 110
- Carbohydrates: 2.4g
- Protein: 4g

COCONUT FLOUR BREAD

Servings: **12 pcs**

Preparation time: **10 minutes**

Cook time: : **15 minutes**

Ingredients

- 6 eggs
- 1/2 cup coconut flour
- 2 tbsp psyllium husk
- 1/4 cup olive oil
- 1 1/2 tsp salt
- 1 tbsp xanthan gum
- 1 tbsp baking powder
- 2 1/4 tsp yeast

Directions

1. Use a small bowl to combine all of the dry ingredients except for the yeast.
2. In the bread machine pan, add all the wet ingredients.
3. Add all of your dry ingredients from the small mixing bowl to the bread machine pan. Top with the yeast.
4. Set the machine to the basic setting.
5. When the bread is finished, remove the bread machine pan from the bread machine.
6. Let cool slightly before transferring to a cooling rack.
7. It can be stored for four days on the counter and up to 3

months in the freezer.

Nutrition Information

- Calories: 174
- Carbohydrates: 4g
- Protein: 7g
- Fat: 15g

FLAX BREAD

Ingredients

- ¾ cup of water
- 200 g ground flax seeds
- ½ cup psyllium husk powder
- 1 Tbsp. baking powder
- Seven large egg whites
- 3 Tbsp. butter
- 2 tsp. salt
- ¼ cup granulated stevia
- One large whole egg

Directions

1. Preheat the oven to 350F.
2. Combine whey protein isolate, psyllium husk, baking powder, sweetener, and salt.
3. In another bowl, mix the water, butter, egg and egg whites.
4. Slowly add psyllium husk mixture to egg mixture and mix well.
5. Grease the pan lightly with butter and pour in the batter.
6. Bake in the oven until the bread is set, about 18 to 20 minutes.

- 1 ½ cups whey
  protein isolate

Nutrition Information

- Calories: 265.5
- Fat: 15.68g
- Carb: 1.88g
- Protein:24.34 g

WARM SPICED PUMPKIN BREAD

Servings: One loaf (12 slices)

Preparation time: 10 minutes

Cook time: : 60 to 75 minutes

Ingredients

- 1½ cups pumpkin purée
- Three eggs, at room temperature
- 1/3 cup melted butter cooled
- 1 cup of sugar
- 3 cups all-purpose flour

Directions

1. Lightly grease the bread bucket with butter.
2. Add the pumpkin, eggs, butter, and sugar.
3. Program the machine for Quick/Rapid setting and press Start.
4. Let the wet ingredients be mixed by the paddles until the first fast mixing cycle is finished, about 10 minutes into the process.
5. While the wet ingredients are mixing stir together the flour, baking powder, cinnamon, baking

- 1½ teaspoons baking powder
- ¾ teaspoon ground cinnamon
- ½ teaspoon baking soda
- ¼ teaspoon ground nutmeg
- ¼ teaspoon ground ginger
- ¼ teaspoon salt
- Pinch ground cloves

soda, nutmeg ginger, salt, and cloves until well blended.

6. Add the dry ingredients to the bucket when the second fast mixing cycle starts.

7. Scrape down the sides of the bucket once after the dry ingredients are mixed into the wet.

8. When the loaf is finished, remove the bucket from the machine.

9. Let it cool for five minutes.

10. Gently shake the bucket to remove the bread and turn it out onto a rack to cool.

Nutrition Information

- Calories: 251
- Fat: 7g
- Carbohydrates: 43g
- Fibre: 2g
- Sodium: 159mg
- Protein: 5g

MULTIGRAIN BREAD

Servings: 8 slices

Preparation time: 15 minutes

Cook time: : 35 minutes

Ingredients

- ¾ cups of water, at 80°F to 90°F
- One tablespoon melted butter cooled
- ½ tablespoon honey
- ½ teaspoon salt
- ¾ cup multigrain flour
- 1 1/3 cups white bread flour

Directions

1. Place the ingredients in the device as recommended by the manufacturer.
2. Program the machine for a Basic White bread, select light or medium crust, then press the Start button.
3. When the loaf is finished, remove the bucket from the machine.
4. Let it cool for five minutes.
5. Gently shake the bucket to remove the bread and turn it out onto a rack to cool.

- One teaspoon bread machine or active dry yeast

Nutrition Information

- Calories: 145
- Fat: 2g
- Carbohydrates: 27g
- Fibre: 1g
- Sodium: 305mg
- Protein: 4g

WHOLE-WHEAT SEED BREAD

Servings: 8 slices

Preparation time: 15 minutes

Cook time: : 40-50 minutes

Ingredients

- ¾ cup of water, at 80°F to 90°F
- One tablespoon honey
- One tablespoon melted butter cooled
- ½ teaspoon salt
- 2 cups whole-wheat flour
- ½ cup white bread flour
- Two tablespoons raw

Directions

1. Place the ingredients in your machine as recommended by the manufacturer.

2. Program the machine for Whole-Wheat/Whole-Grain bread. Select light or medium crust, press the Start button.

3. When the loaf is finished, remove the bucket from the machine.

4. Let it cool for 5 minutes.

5. Gently shake the bucket to remove the bread and turn it out onto a rack to cool.

sunflower seeds

- One tablespoon
  sesame seeds

- One teaspoon bread
  machine or instant
  yeast

Nutrition Information

- Calories: 157 Cal
- Fat: 3 g
- Carbohydrates: 39 g

Chapter 2: Bread with herbs

GARLIC, HERB, AND CHEESE BREAD

Servings: One loaf (12 slices)

Preparation time: **2 hours**

Cook time: : **15 minutes**

Ingredients

- 1/2 cup ghee
- Six eggs
- 2 cups almond flour
- 1 tbsp baking powder
- 1/2 tsp xanthan gum
- 1 cup cheddar cheese, shredded
- 1 tbsp garlic powder

Directions

1. Lightly beat eggs and ghee before pouring into bread machine pan.
2. Add the remaining ingredients to the pan.
3. Set bread machine to gluten-free.
4. When the bread is finished, remove the bread pan from the bread machine.
5. Let it cool for a while before transferring into a cooling rack.

- 1 tbsp parsley
- 1/2 tbsp oregano
- 1/2 tsp salt

6. You can store your bread for up to 5 days in the refrigerator.

Nutrition Information

- Calories: 156
- Carbohydrates: 4g
- Protein: 5g
- Fat: 13g

SAVOURY HERB BLEND BREAD

Servings: 16 pcs

Preparation time: 20 minutes

Cook time: : One hour

Ingredients

- 1 cup almond flour
- 1/2 cup coconut flour
- 1 cup parmesan cheese
- 3/4 tsp baking powder
- Three eggs
- 3 tbsp coconut oil
- 1/2 tbsp rosemary
- 1/2 tsp thyme,

Directions

1. Light beat eggs and coconut oil together before adding to the bread machine pan.
2. Add all the remaining ingredients to the bread machine pan.
3. Set the bread machine to the gluten-free setting.
4. When the bread is finished, remove the bread
5. machine pan from the bread machine.
6. Let cool slightly before transferring to a cooling rack.
7. You can store your bread for up to 7 days.

ground

- 1/2 tsp sage, ground
- 1/2 tsp oregano
- 1/2 tsp garlic powder
- 1/2 tsp onion powder
- 1/4 tsp salt

Nutrition Information

- Calories: 170
- Carbohydrates: 6g
- Protein: 9g
- Fat: 15g

SEMOLINA BREAD

Servings: 6 pcs

Preparation time: 20 minutes

Cook time: : One hour

Ingredients

- Almond fine flour, one cup
- Semolina flour, one cup
- Yeast, one teaspoon
- An egg
- Salt, one teaspoon
- Stevia powder, two teaspoons
- Olive oil extra virgin,

Directions

1. Get a mixing container and combine the almond flour, semolina flour, salt, and stevia powder.

2. In another mixing container, combine the egg extra virgin olive oil, and warm water.

3. By instructions on your machine's manual, pour the ingredients in the bread pan and follow how to mix in the yeast.

4. Put the bread pan in the machine, select the basic bread setting together with the bread size and crust type, if available,

two teaspoons

- Water warm, one cup
- Sesame seeds, two teaspoons

then press start once you have closed the machine's lid.

5. When the bread is ready, open the lid and spread the sesame seeds at the top and close for a few minutes.

6. By using oven mitts, remove the pan from the machine. Use a stainless spatula to extract the pan's bread and turn the pan upside down on a metallic rack where the bread will cool off before slicing it.

Nutrition Information

- Calories: 100
- Carbohydrates: 2.8g
- Protein: 5g
- Fat: 14g

SEEDED BREAD

Servings: 16 slices

Preparation time: 30 minutes

Cook time: : 40 minutes

Ingredients

- Two tablespoons chia seeds
- 1/4 teaspoon salt
- Seven large eggs
- 1/2 teaspoon xanthan gum
- 2 cups almond flour
- One teaspoon baking powder
- 1/2 cup unsalted butter

Directions

1. Add all the ingredients to the Bread machine.
2. Close the lid and choose Bread mode. Once done, take out from the machine and cut into at least 16 slices.
3. This seeded bread can be kept for up to 4-5 days in the fridge.

- Three tablespoons sesame seeds
- Two tablespoons olive oil

Nutrition Information

- Calories: 101 Cal
- Fat: 4 g
- Cholesterol:
- Carbohydrates: 4 g
- Protein: 6 g

MACADAMIA BREAD

Servings: 8 pcs

Preparation time: 30 minutes

Cook time: : 60 minutes

Ingredients

- ¼ cup almond flour
- 1 cup macadamia nuts
- Two tablespoons flax meal
- One teaspoon baking powder
- Two scoops of whey protein powder
- Four eggs

Directions

1. Add all the ingredients to the Bread machine.
2. Close the lid and choose Express Bake mode. Once done, take out from the machine and cut into at least 16 slices.

- Two egg whites
- One tablespoon lemon juice
- ¼ cup butter, melted

Nutrition Information

- Calories: 257 Cal
- Fat: 22.4g
- Carbohydrates: 4.5g
- Protein: 11.5g

ORANGE ALMOND BACON BREAD

Servings: 10 pcs

Preparation time: 3 hours 18 minutes

Cook time: : 60 minutes

Ingredients

- 1 ½ cups almond flour
- One tablespoon baking powder
- 7 oz bacon, diced
- Two eggs
- 1 ½ cups cheddar cheese, shredded
- Four tablespoons

Directions

1. Add all ingredients to the bread machine.
2. Close the lid and choose the Sweet Bread mode.
3. After the cooking time is over, remove the machine's bread and rest for about 10 minutes.
4. Enjoy!

butter, melted
- 1/3 cup sour cream

Nutrition Information

- Calories: 307 Cal
- Fat: 26 g
- Carbohydrate:3 g
- Protein: 14 g

ROSEMARY GARLIC DINNER ROLLS

Servings: 10 pcs

Preparation time: 10 minutes

Cook time: : 30 minutes

Ingredients

- ½ teaspoon baking powder
- 1/3 cup ground flax seed
- 1 cup mozzarella cheese, shredded
- 1 cup almond flour
- One teaspoon rosemary, minced

Directions

1. Add all ingredients to the Bread Machine.
2. Select Dough setting. When the time is over, transfer the dough to the floured surface. Shape it into a ball.
3. Roll the dough until it becomes a log and slice into six slices. Place on a greased baking sheet.
4. Combine rosemary, garlic, and butter in a bowl and mix—brush half of this over the biscuits.
5. Set the heat of the oven to 400F and bake for 15 minutes.

- A pinch of salt
- 1 oz. cream cheese
- One egg
  beaten
- One tablespoon butter
- One teaspoon garlic,
  minced

6. Brush with the remaining mixture and add salt before serving.

Nutrition Information

- Calories: 168 Cal
- Fat: 12.9g
- Carbohydrates: 5.4g
- Protein: 10.3g

EGG AND SEED BUNS

Servings: 8 pcs

Preparation time: **10 minutes**

Cook time: : **50 minutes**

Ingredients

- Two egg whites
- 1 cup sunflower seeds, ground
- ¼ cup flax seeds, ground
- 5 Tbsp. psyllium husks
- 1 cup boiling water
- 2 tsp. baking powder
- Salt to taste

Directions

1. Combine all the dry ingredients.
2. Add the egg whites and blend until smooth.
3. Add boiling water and keep whisking.
4. Line a baking sheet with parchment paper and drop the dough on it one spoonful at a time to form buns.
5. Bake at 356F for 50 minutes.
6. Serve.

Nutrition Information

- Calories: 91 Cal
- Fat: 4.2g
- Carb: 12.1g
- Protein: 3.3g

COCO-CILANTRO FLATBREAD

Servings: 6 pcs

Preparation time: **10 minutes**

Cook time: : **15 minutes**

Ingredients

- ½ cup Coconut Flour
- 2 tbsp. Flax Meal
- ¼ tsp Baking Soda
- pinch of Salt
- 1 tbsp. Coconut Oil
- 2 tbsp. Chopped Cilantro
- 1 cup Lukewarm Water

Directions

1. Whisk together the coconut flour, flax, baking soda, and salt in a bowl.
2. Add in the water, coconut oil, and chopped cilantro.
3. Knead it until everything comes together into a smooth dough.
4. Leave to rest for about 15 minutes.
5. Divide the dough into six equal-sized portions.
6. Roll each of it into a ball, then flatten with a rolling pin in between sheets of parchment paper.
7. Refrigerate until ready to use.

8. To cook, heat in a non-stick pan for 2-3 minutes per side.

Nutrition Information

- Kcal per serve: 46
- Fat: 4 g. (84%)
- Protein: 1 g. (3%)
- Carbs: 1 g. (13%)

PARSLEY CHEDDAR BREAD

Servings: 2 pcs

Preparation time: 10 minutes

Cook time: : 4 minutes

Ingredients

- 1 tbsp butter
- 2 tbsp coconut flour
- One large egg
- 1 tbsp heavy whipping cream
- 2 tbsp water
- 1/4 cup cheddar cheese
- 1/8 tsp garlic powder
- 1/8 tsp onion powder

Directions

1. Melt the butter by heating on a coffee mug for 20 seconds.
2. Slowly stir in seasonings, baking powder, and coconut flour. Mix well using a fork until smooth.
3. Whisk in cream, cheese, water, and egg.
4. Beat well until smooth, then bake for 3 minutes in the microwave.
5. Allow the bread to cool, then serve.

- 1/8 tsp dried parsley
- 1/8 tsp pink
  Himalayan salt
- 1/8 tsp black pepper
- 1/4 tsp baking
  powder

Nutrition Information

- Calories 113
- Total Fat 8.4 g
- Saturated Fat 12.1 g
- Cholesterol 27 mg
- Sodium 39 mg

  Total Carbs 9.2 g
- Sugar 3.1 g Fiber 4.6 g
- Protein 8.1 g

LAVENDER BREAD

Ingredients

- ¾ cup lukewarm milk (80 degrees F)
- One tablespoon butter, melted
- One tablespoon brown sugar
- ¾ teaspoon salt
- One teaspoon fresh lavender flower, chopped

Directions

1. Prepare all of the ingredients for your bread and measuring means (a cup, a spoon, kitchen scales).
2. Carefully measure the ingredients into the pan.
3. Place all of the ingredients into a bucket in the right order, following the manual for your bread machine.
4. Close the cover.
5. Select the program of your bread machine to BASIC and choose the crust colour to MEDIUM.
6. Press START.

- ¼ teaspoon lemon zest
- ¼ teaspoon fresh thyme, chopped
- 2 cups all-purpose flour, sifted
- ¾ teaspoon active dry yeast

7. Wait until the program completes.
8. When done, take the bucket out and let it cool for 5-10 minutes.
9. Shake the loaf from the pan and let cool for 30 minutes on a cooling rack.
10. Slice, serve and enjoy the taste of fragrant Homemade Bread.

Nutrition Information

- Calories 133
- Total Fat 1.8g
- Saturated Fat 1g
- Cholesterol 4g
- Sodium 228mg
- Total Carbohydrate 25.3g
- Dietary Fiber 0.9g
- Total Sugars 1.2g
- Protein 3.4g
- Potassium 43mg

ONION BACON BREAD

Servings: 22 slices

Preparation time: 2 hours

Cook time: : 1 hour

Ingredients

- 1 ½ cups lukewarm water (80 degrees F)
- Two tablespoons sugar
- Three teaspoons active dry yeast
- 4 ½ cups wheat flour
- One whole egg
- Two teaspoons kosher

Directions

1. Prepare all of the ingredients for your bread and measuring means (a cup, a spoon, kitchen scales).

2. Carefully measure the ingredients into the pan, except the bacon and onion.

3. Place all of the ingredients into a bucket in the right order, following the manual for your bread machine.

4. Close the cover.

5. Select the program of your bread machine to BASIC and

- salt
- One tablespoon olive oil
- Three small onions, chopped and lightly toasted
- 1 cup bacon, chopped

choose the crust colour to MEDIUM.

6. Press START.
7. After the machine beeps, add the onion and bacon.
8. Wait until the program completes.
9. When done, take the bucket out and let it cool for 5-10 minutes.
10. Shake the loaf from the pan and let cool for 30 minutes on a cooling rack.
11. Slice, serve and enjoy the taste of fragrant Homemade Bread.

Nutrition Information

- Calories: 391 Cal
- Fat: 9.7 g
- Cholesterol: 38 g
- Sodium: 960 mg
- Carbohydrates: 59.9 g
- Total Sugars 1.2g
- Protein 3.4g
- Potassium 43mg

Chapter 3: Bread with Cheese

ONION, GARLIC, CHEESE BREAD

Servings: One loaf

Preparation time: **50 minutes**

Cook time: : **40 minutes**

Ingredients

- Three tablespoons dried minced onion
- 3 cups bread flour
- Two teaspoons Garlic powder
- Two teaspoons Active

Directions

1. In the order suggested by the manufacturer, put the flour, water, powdered milk, margarine or butter, salt, and yeast in the bread pan.

2. Press the basic cycle with a light crust. When the manufacturer directs the sound alerts, add two teaspoons of the onion flakes, the garlic powder, and shredded

dry yeast

- Two tablespoons White sugar
- Two tablespoons Margarine
- Two tablespoons Dry milk powder
- 1 cup shredded sharp cheddar cheese
- 1 1/8 cups warm water
- 1 1/2 teaspoon salt

cheese.

3. After the last kneed, sprinkle the remaining onion flakes over the dough.

Nutrition Information

- Calories: 204 calories
- Total Carbohydrate: 29 g
- Total Fat: 6 g
- Protein: 8 g

CREAM CHEESE BREAD

Servings: 1 loaf

Preparation time: 60 minutes

Cook time: : 35 minutes

Ingredients

- 1/2 cup Water
- 1/2 cup Cream cheese, softened
- Two tablespoons melted butter
- 1 Beaten egg
- Four tablespoons Sugar
- One teaspoon salt

Directions

1. Place the ingredients in the pan in order, as suggested by your bread machine.
2. After removing it from a machine, place it in a greased 9x5 loaf pan after the cycle.
3. Cover and let rise until doubled.
4. Bake in a 350° oven for approximately 35 minutes.

- 3 cups bread flour
- 1 1/2 teaspoons
  Active dry yeast

Nutrition Information

- Calories: 150 calories
- Total Carbohydrate: 24 g
- Total Fat: 5 g
- Protein: 3 g

MOZZARELLA CHEESE AND SALAMI LOAF

Servings: 1 loaf

Preparation time: **2 hours and 50 minutes**

Cook time: : 45 minutes

Ingredients

- ¾ cup water, set at 80 degrees F
- 1/3 cup mozzarella cheese, shredded
- Four teaspoons sugar
- 2/3 teaspoon salt
- 2/3 teaspoon dried

Directions

1. Add the listed ingredients to your bread machine (except salami), following the manufactures instructions.
2. Set the bread machine's program to Basic/White Bread and the crust type to light. Press Start.
3. Let the bread machine work and wait until it beeps. This your indication to add the remaining ingredients at this point, add the salami.

- basil
- Pinch of garlic powder
- 2 cups + 2 tablespoons white bread flour
- One teaspoon instant yeast
- ½ cup hot salami, finely diced

4. Wait until the remaining bake cycle completes.
5. Once the loaf is done, take the bucket out from the bread machine and let it rest for 5 minutes.
6. Gently shake the bucket and remove the loaf, transfer the loaf to a cooling rack and slice.
7. Serve and enjoy!

Nutrition Information

- Calories: 164 calories
- Total Carbohydrate: 28 g
- Total Fat: 3 g
- Protein: 6 g
- Sugar: 2 g

OLIVE AND CHEDDAR LOAF

Servings: 1 loaf

Preparation time: 2 hours and 50 minutes

Cook time: : 45 minutes

Ingredients

- 1 cup water, room temperature
- Four teaspoons sugar
- ¾ teaspoon salt
- 1 and 1/ cups sharp cheddar cheese, shredded
- 3 cups bread flour
- Two teaspoons active dry yeast

Directions

1. Add the listed ingredients to your bread machine (except salami), following the manufactures instructions.

2. Set the bread machine's program to Basic/White Bread and the crust type to light. Press Start.

3. Let the bread machine work and wait until it beeps this your indication to add the remaining ingredients. At this point, add the salami.

4. Wait until the remaining bake cycle completes.

5. Once the loaf is done, take the bucket out from the bread machine and let it rest for 5 minutes.

- ¾ cup pimiento olives, drained and sliced

6. Gently shake the bucket and remove the loaf, transfer the loaf to a cooling rack and slice.

7. Serve and enjoy!

Nutrition Information

- Calories: 124 calories
- Total Carbohydrate: 19 g
- Total Fat: 4 g
- Protein: 5 g
- Sugar: 5 g

COTTAGE CHEESE BREAD

Servings: 1 loaf

Preparation time: **2 hours and 50 minutes**

Cook time: : **45 minutes**

Ingredients

- 1/2 cup water
- 1 cup cottage cheese
- Two tablespoons margarine
- One egg
- One tablespoon white sugar
- 1/4 teaspoon baking soda
- One teaspoon salt

Directions

1. Into the bread machine, place the ingredients according to the ingredients list's order, then push the start button. In case the dough looks too sticky, feel free to use up to half a cup more bread flour.

- 3 cups bread flour
- 2 1/2 teaspoons active dry yeast

Nutrition Information

- Calories: 171 calories
- Total Carbohydrate: 26.8 g
- Cholesterol: 18 mg
- Total Fat: 3.6 g
- Protein: 7.3 g
- Sodium: 324 mg

GREEN CHEESE BREAD

Servings: 8 pcs

Preparation time: **3 hours**

Cook time: : **15 minutes**

Ingredients

- ¾ cup lukewarm water
- 1 Tablespoon sugar
- One teaspoon kosher salt
- 2 Tablespoon green cheese
- 1 cup of wheat bread machine flour
- 9/10 cup whole-grain

Directions

1. Place all the dry and liquid ingredients, except paprika, in the pan and follow the instructions for your bread machine.

2. Pay particular attention to measuring the ingredients. Use a measuring cup, measuring spoon, and kitchen scales to do so.

3. Dissolve yeast in warm milk with a saucepan and add in the last turn.

4. Add paprika after the beep or place it in the dispenser of the bread machine.

flour, finely ground

- One teaspoon bread machine yeast
- One teaspoon ground paprika

5. Set the baking program to BASIC and the crust type to DARK.

6. If the dough is too wet, adjust the recipe's amount of flour and liquid.

7. When the program has ended, take the pan out of the bread machine and cool for 5 minutes.

8. Shake the loaf out of the pan. If necessary, use a spatula.

9. Wrap the bread with a kitchen towel and set it aside for an hour. Otherwise, you can cool it on a wire rack.

Nutrition Information

- Calories: 118 calories
- Total Carbohydrate: 23.6 g
- Cholesterol: 2 g
- Total Fat: 1 g
- Protein: 4.1 g
- Sodium: 304 mg
- Sugar: 1.6 g

CHEESY CHIPOTLE BREAD

Servings: 8 pcs

Preparation time: **2 hours**

Cook time: : **15 minutes**

Ingredients

- 2/3 cup water, set at 80°F to 90°F
- 1½ tablespoons sugar
- 1½ tablespoons powdered skim milk
- ¾ teaspoon salt
- ½ teaspoon chipotle chilli powder
- 2 cups white bread flour

Directions

1. Place the ingredients in your machine as recommended on it.
2. Make a program on the machine for basic white Bread, select Light or medium crust, and press Start.
3. When the loaf is finished, remove the bucket from the machine.
4. Let the loaf cool for a minute.
5. Gently shake the bucket and remove the loaf and turn it out onto a rack to cool.

- ½ cup (2 ounces) shredded sharp Cheddar cheese
- ¾ teaspoon instant yeast

Nutrition Information

- Calories: 139 calories
- Total Carbohydrate: 27 g
- Total Fat: 1g
- Protein: 6 g
- Sodium: 245 mg

CHEDDAR CHEESE BASIL BREAD

Servings: 8 pcs

Preparation time: **2 hours**

Cook time: : **15 minutes**

Ingredients

- 2/3 cup milk, set at 80°F to 90°F
- Two teaspoons melted butter, cooled
- Two teaspoons sugar
- 2/3 teaspoon dried basil
- ½ cup (2 ounces) shredded sharp Cheddar cheese

Directions

1. Place the ingredients in your machine as recommended on it.
2. Make a Program on the machine for basic white Bread, select Light or medium crust, and press Start.
3. When the loaf is finished, remove the bucket from the machine.
4. Let the loaf cool for a minute.
5. Gently shake the bucket and remove the loaf and turn it out onto a rack to cool.

- ½ teaspoon salt
- 2 cups white bread flour
- One teaspoon active dry yeast.

Nutrition Information

- Calories: 166 calories
- Total Carbohydrate: 26 g
- Total Fat: 4g
- Protein: 6 g
- Sodium: 209 mg

OLIVE CHEESE BREAD

Servings: 8 pcs

Preparation time: **2 hours**

Cook time: : **15 minutes**

Ingredients

- 2/3 cup milk, set at 80°F to 90°F
- One tablespoon melted butter cooled
- 2/3 Teaspoon minced garlic
- One tablespoon sugar
- 2/3 teaspoon salt
- 2 cups white bread

Directions

1. Place the ingredients in your device as recommended on it.
2. Make a program on the machine for basic white Bread, select Light or medium crust, and press Start.
3. When the loaf is finished, remove the bucket from the machine.
4. Let the loaf cool for a minute.
5. Gently shake the bucket and remove the loaf and turn it out onto a rack to cool.

flour

- ½ cup (2 ounces) shredded Swiss cheese
- ¾ teaspoon bread machine or instant yeast
- ¼ cup chopped black olives

Nutrition Information

- Calories: 175 calories
- Total Carbohydrate: 27 g
- Total Fat: 5g
- Protein: 6 g
- Sodium: 260 mg

DOUBLE CHEESE BREAD

Ingredients

- ¾ cup plus one tablespoon milk, at 80°F to 90°F
- Two teaspoons butter, melted and cooled
- Four teaspoons sugar
- 2/3 teaspoon salt
- 1/3 teaspoon freshly ground black pepper
- Pinch cayenne pepper

Directions

1. Place the ingredients in your machine as recommended on it.
2. Make a program on the machine for Basic White bread, select light or medium crust, and press Start.
3. When the loaf is finished, remove the bucket from the machine.
4. Let the loaf cool for a minute.
5. Gently shake the bucket and remove the loaf and turn it out onto a rack to cool.

- 1 cup (4 ounces) shredded aged sharp Cheddar cheese
- 1/3 cup shredded or grated Parmesan cheese
- 2 cups white bread flour
- ¾ teaspoon instant yeast

Nutrition Information

- Calories: 183 calories
- Total Carbohydrate: 28 g
- Total Fat: 4g
- Protein: 6 g
- Sodium: 344 mg

CHILE CHEESE BACON BREAD

Servings: 8 pcs

Preparation time: **2 hours**

Cook time: : **15 minutes**

Ingredients

- 1/3 cup milk, set at 80°F to 90°F
- One teaspoon melted butter cooled
- One tablespoon honey
- One teaspoon salt
- 1/3 cup chopped and drained green Chile
- 1/3 cup grated Cheddar cheese
- 1/3 cup chopped cooked bacon

Directions

1. Place the ingredients in your device as recommended on it.
2. Make a program on the machine for basic white Bread, select Light or medium crust, and press Start.
3. When the loaf is finished, remove the bucket from the machine.
4. Let the loaf cool for a minute.
5. Gently shake the bucket and remove the loaf and turn it out onto a rack to cool.

- 2 cups white bread flour
- 1 1/3 teaspoons bread machine or instant yeast

Nutrition Information

- Calories: 174 calories
- Total Carbohydrate: 404 g
- Total Fat: 4 g
- Protein: 6 g
- Sodium: 1 mg

ITALIAN PARMESAN BREAD

Servings: 8 pcs

Preparation time: **2 hours**

Cook time: : **15 minutes**

Ingredients

- ¾ cup water, set at 80°F to 90°F
- Two tablespoons melted butter
- Two teaspoons sugar
- 2/3 teaspoon salt
- 1 1/3 teaspoons chopped fresh basil
- 2 2/3 tablespoons

Directions

1. Place the ingredients in your device as recommended on it.
2. Make a program on the machine for Basic White bread, select light or medium crust, and press Start.
3. When it's finished, remove the bucket from the machine.
4. Let the loaf cool for a minute.
5. Gently shake the bucket and remove the loaf and turn it out onto a rack to cool.

grated Parmesan
cheese

- 2 1/3 cups white bread
  flour
- One teaspoon bread
  machine or instant
  yeast

Nutrition Information

- Calories: 171 calories
- Total Carbohydrate: 29 g
- Total Fat: 4 g
- Protein: 5 g
- Sodium: 237 mg

FETA OREGANO BREAD

Servings: 8 pcs

Preparation time: **2 hours**

Cook time: : **15 minutes**

Ingredients

- 2/3 Cup of milk, at 80°F to 90°F
- Two teaspoons melted butter, cooled
- Two teaspoons sugar
- 2/3 teaspoon salt
- Two teaspoons dried oregano
- 2 cups white bread flour
- 1½ teaspoons bread machine or instant yeast
- 2/3 cup (2½ ounces)

Directions

1. Place the ingredients in your device as recommended on it.
2. Make a program on the machine for Basic White bread, select light or medium crust, and press Start.
3. When it's finished, remove the bucket from the machine.
4. Let the loaf cool for a minute.
5. Gently shake the bucket and remove the loaf and turn it out onto a rack to cool.

crumbled feta cheese

Nutrition Information

- Calories: 164 Cal
- Carbohydrates: 27 g
- Fat: 4g
- Protein: 5

Chapter 4: Vegetable Bread

SUN VEGETABLE BREAD

Servings: 8 pcs

Preparation time: **2 hours and 30 minutes**

Cook time: : **1 hour and 30 minutes**

Ingredients

- 2 cups (250 g) wheat flour
- 2 cups (250 g) whole-wheat flour
- Two teaspoons yeast
- 1½ teaspoons salt

Directions

1. The set baking program, which should be 4 hours, crust colour, is medium.

2. Be sure to look at the kneading phase of the dough to get a smooth and soft bun.

- One tablespoon sugar
- One tablespoon paprika dried slices
- Two tablespoons dried beets
- One tablespoon dried garlic
- 1½ cups water
- One tablespoon vegetable oil

Nutrition Information

- Calories 253
- Total Fat 2.6g
- Saturated Fat 0.5g
- Cholesterol 0g
- Sodium 444mg
- Total Sugars 0.6g
- Protein 7.2g

TOMATO ONION BREAD

Servings: 12 slices

Preparation time: 2 hours and 30 minutes

Cook time: : 1 hour and 30 minutes

Ingredients

- 2 cups all-purpose flour
- 1 cup wholemeal flour
- ½ cup of warm water
- 4¾ ounces (140 ml) milk
- Three tablespoons olive oil
- Two tablespoons sugar
- One teaspoon salt
- Two teaspoons dry

Directions

1. Prepare all the necessary products. Finely chop the onion and sauté in a frying pan. Cut up the sun-dried tomatoes (10 halves).

2. Pour all liquid ingredients into the bowl, then cover with flour and put in the tomatoes and onions. Pour in the yeast and baking powder without touching the liquid.

3. Select the baking mode and start. You can choose the Bread with Additives program, and then the bread maker will knead the dough at low speeds. I chose the usual baking mode
the kneading was very active, and the vegetables practically dissolved in the dough. For children who like to find something in the food and carefully remove it from it

yeast

- ½ teaspoon baking powder
- Five sun-dried tomatoes
- One onion
- ¼ teaspoon black pepper

(for example, pieces of onions), this is an ideal option!

4. Enjoy!

Nutrition Information

- Calories 241
- Total Fat 6.4g
- Saturated Fat 1.1g
- Sodium 305mg
- Total Carbohydrate 40g
- Total Sugars 6.8g
- Protein 6.7g

TOMATO BREAD

Servings: 8 pcs

Preparation time: **2 hours**

Cook time: : **1 hour and 30 minutes**

Ingredients

- Three tablespoons tomato paste
- 1½ cups (340 ml) water
- 4 1/3 cups (560 g) flour
- 1½ tablespoon vegetable oil
- Two teaspoons sugar
- Two teaspoons salt

Directions

1. Dilute the tomato paste in warm water. If you do not like the tomato flavour, reduce the amount of tomato paste, but putting less than one tablespoon does not make sense because the colour will fade.

2. Prepare the spices. I added a little more oregano and Provencal herbs to the oregano and paprika (this bread also begs for kicks).

3. Sift the flour to enrich it with oxygen. Add the spices to the flour and mix well.

4. Pour the vegetable oil into the bread maker container. Add

- 1 ½ teaspoons dry yeast
- ½ teaspoon oregano, dried
- ½ teaspoon ground sweet paprika

the tomato/water mixture, sugar, salt, the flour with spices, and then the yeast. Turn on the bread maker (the Basic program – I have the WHITE BREAD – the crust Medium).

5. After the end of the baking cycle, turn off the bread maker. Remove the bread container and take out the hot bread. Place it on the grate for cooling for 1 hour.

6. Enjoy!

Nutrition Information

- Calories 281
- Total Fat 3.3g
- Saturated Fat 0.6g
- Cholesterol 0g
- Sodium 590mg
- Total Carbohydrate 54.3g
- Dietary Fiber 2.4g
- Total Sugars 1.9g
- Protein 7.6g

CURD ONION BREAD WITH SESAME SEEDS

Servings: 8 pcs

Preparation time: 2 hours and 30 minutes

Cook time: : 1 hour and 30 minutes

Ingredients

- ¾ cup of water
- 3 2/3 cups wheat flour
- ¾ cup cottage cheese
- Two tablespoons softened butter
- Two tablespoon sugar

Directions

1. Put the products in the bread maker according to its instructions.
2. Bake on the BASIC program.

- 1 ½ teaspoons salt
- 1 ½ tablespoon sesame seeds
- Two tablespoons dried onions
- One ¼ teaspoons dry yeast

Nutrition Information

- Calories 277
- Total Fat 4.7g
- Saturated Fat 2.3g
- Cholesterol 9g
- Sodium 547mg
- Total Carbohydrate 48.4g
- Dietary Fiber 1.9g
- Total Sugars 3.3g
- Protein 9.4g

SQUASH CARROT BREAD

Servings: 8 pcs

Preparation time: **2 hours and 30 minutes**

Cook time: : **1 hour and 30 minutes**

Ingredients

- One small zucchini
- One baby carrot
- 1 cup whey
- 1 ½ cups (180 g) white wheat flour
- ¾ cup (100 g) whole

Directions

1. Cut/dice carrots and zucchini to about 8-10 mm (1/2 inch) in size.

2. In a frying pan, heat the vegetable oil, then fry the vegetables over medium heat until soft. If desired, season the vegetables with salt and pepper.

3. Transfer the vegetables to a flat plate so that they cool

wheat flour

- ¾ cup (100 g) rye flour
- Two tablespoons vegetable oil
- One teaspoon yeast, fresh
- One teaspoon salt
- ½ teaspoon sugar

down more quickly. While still hot, they cannot be added to the dough.

4. Now dissolve the yeast in the serum.

5. Send all kinds of flour, serum with yeast, as well as salt and sugar to the bakery.

6. Knead the dough in the dough for the Rolls program.

7. At the very end of the batch, add the vegetables to the dough.

8. After adding vegetables, the dough will become moister at the end of the fermentation, which will last about an hour before doubling the dough's volume, shift it onto a thickly floured surface.

9. Form into a loaf and put it in an oiled form.

10. Cover the form with a food film and leave for 1 to 1 1/3 hours.

11. Preheat oven to 450°F and put bread in it.

12. Bake the bread for 15 minutes, and then gently remove it from the mould. Lay it on the grate and bake for 15-20 minutes more

Nutrition Information

- Calories 220
- Total Fat 4.3g
- Saturated Fat 0.8g
- Cholesterol 0g
- Sodium 313mg
- Total Carbohydrate 39.1g
- Dietary Fiber 4.1g
- Total Sugars 2.7g
- Protein 6.6g

AUSTRALIAN VEGETABLE BREAD

Servings: 8 pcs

Preparation time: **2 hours**

Cook time: : **1 hour and 50 minutes**

Ingredients

- 4 cups (4 * 1 cup) all-purpose flour
- 4 tablespoons (4 * 1 tbsp) sugar
- 2 teaspoons (4 * ½ tsp) salt
- 2 tablespoons (4 * ½ tbsp) olive oil
- 1 teaspoon (4 * ¼ tsp) yeast
- liquid (3 parts juice +

Directions

1. Knead in the bread maker four types of dough (3 species with different colors with juice and one kind with water). Take juices of mixed vegetables for colored liquid: for Bordeaux - juice of beet
for red color - tomato juice
for green color - juice or puree of spinach
for white dough - water.

2. While the following kind of dough is kneaded, the previous lump stands warm to raise.

3. Use the Pasta Dough program on your bread maker.

4. The finished white dough was rolled into a large cake, the

1-part water)

color dough of each kind was divided into four pieces each. In a white cake, lay the colored scones: roll them into small rolls and wrap them in 3 layers in a different order - you get four rolls. Then completely cover the colored cakes with white dough, create the desired form for the bucket, put it in the bread machine.

5. The program BAKING set the time to 60 minutes. The focus was that the loaf resembles plain white bread (as if bread with a surprise)
However, the colored dough was foolish and sometimes decided to get out.

Nutrition Information

- Calories 225
- Total Fat 3.3g
- Saturated Fat 0.5g
- Cholesterol 0g
- Sodium 466mg
- Total Carbohydrate 43.1g
- Dietary Fiber 1.4g

OLIVE BREAD WITH ITALIAN HERBS

Servings: 8 pcs

Preparation time: **2 hours**

Cook time: : **1 hour and 50 minutes**

Ingredients

- 1 cup (250 ml) water
- ½ cup brine from olives
- Four tablespoons butter
- Three tablespoons sugar
- Two teaspoons salt
- 4 cups flour
- Two teaspoons dry

Directions

1. Add all liquid products. Then add the butter.
2. Fill with brine and water.
3. Add salt and sugar. Gently pour in the flour and pour the dry yeast in the corners on top of the flour.
4. Send the form to the bread maker and wait for the signal before the last dough kneading to add the olives and herbs.
5. In the meantime, cut olives into 2-3 parts. After the bread maker signals, add it and the Italian herbs into the dough.
6. Then wait again for the bread maker to signal that the

yeast
- ½ cup olives
- One teaspoon Italian herbs

bread is ready.

7. Cooled Bread has an exciting structure, not to mention the smell and taste. Bon Appetit!

Nutrition Information

- Calories: 332 Cal
- Fat: 7.5 g
- Cholesterol: 15 g
- Sodium: 749 mg
- Carbohydrates: 55.5 g
- Fiber: 3

Chapter 5: Sweet Bread

BUTTERY SWEET BREAD

Servings: 1 loaf

Preparation time: **2 hours**

Cook time: : **1 hour and 15 minutes**

Ingredients

- 1/3 cup water
- ½ cup milk
- ¼ cup of sugar
- One beaten egg
- One teaspoon of salt
- ¼ cup margarine or ¼ cup butter

Directions

1. Put everything in your bread machine pan.
2. Select the white bread setting.
3. Take out the pan when done and set aside for 10 minutes.

- Two teaspoons bread machine yeast
- 3 1/3 cups bread flour

Nutrition Information

- Calories 168
- Carbohydrates: 28g
- Total Fat 5g
- Cholesterol 0mg
- Protein 4g
- Fiber 1g
- Sugars 3g
- Sodium 292mg
- Potassium 50mg

CINNAMON SUGAR BREAD

Servings: 1 loaf

Preparation time: **1 hour and 10 minutes**

Cook time: : **1 hour**

Ingredients

- One pack active dry yeast
- ½ cup of sugar
- 3 cups bread flour
- 1/4 cup cocoa powder
- One large egg
- 1/4 cup butter

Directions

1. Put everything in the pan of your bread machine.
2. Select the quick bread or equivalent setting.
3. Take out the pan when done and set aside for 10 minutes.

- ½ teaspoon vanilla extract
- 1 cup milk

Nutrition Information

- Calories 184
- Carbohydrates: 31g
- Total Fat 5g
- Cholesterol 13mg
- Protein 5g
- Fiber 2g
- Sugar 8g
- Sodium 214mg
- Potassium 92mg

CRANBERRY WALNUT BREAD

Servings: 1 loaf

Preparation time: **1 hour and 10 minutes**

Cook time: : **1 hour**

Ingredients

- ¼ cup of water
- ¼ cup rolled oats
- One egg
- 1 cup buttermilk
- 1-1/2 tablespoons margarine
- Three tablespoons honey

Directions

1. Put everything in your bread machine pan, except the walnuts and cranberries.
2. Set the machine to the light crust and the sweet cycle modes.
3. Hit the start button.
4. Add the walnuts and cranberries at the beep signal.
5. Take out the pan when done and set aside for 10 minutes.

- One teaspoon salt
- 3 cups bread flour
- ½ teaspoon ground cinnamon
- ¼ teaspoon baking soda
- ¾ cup dried cranberries
- Two teaspoons active dry yeast
- ½ cup chopped walnuts

Nutrition Information

- Calories 184
- Carbohydrates: 31g
- Total Fat 5g
- Cholesterol 13mg
- Protein 5g
- Fiber 2g
- Sugar 8g
- Sodium 214mg
- Potassium 92mg

COCONUT GINGER BREAD

Servings: 1 loaf

Preparation time: **1 hour and 10 minutes**

Cook time: : **1 hour**

Ingredients

- 1 cup + 2 tbsp Half & Half
- One ¼ cup toasted shredded coconut
- Two large eggs
- ¼ cup oil
- 1 tsp coconut extract
- 1 tsp lemon extract
- 3/4 cup sugar
- 1 tbsp grated lemon

Directions

1. Put everything in your bread machine pan.
2. Select the quick bread mode.
3. Press the start button.
4. Allow bread to cool on the wire rack until ready to serve (at least 20 minutes).

peel

- 2 cups all-purpose flour
- 2 tbsp finely chopped candied ginger
- 1 tbsp baking powder
- ½ tsp salt
- One ¼ cup toasted shredded coconut

Nutrition Information

- Calories 210
- Carbohydrates: 45g
- Total Fat 3g
- Cholesterol3mg
- Protein 5g
- Fiber 2g
- Sugar 15g
- Sodium 185mg
- Potassium 61mg

EASY DONUTS

Servings: 12

Preparation time: **1 hour and 10 minutes**

Cook time: : **1 hour**

Ingredients

- 2/3 cups milk, room temperature
- 1/4 cup water, room temperature
- ½ cup of warm water
- 1/4 cup softened butter
- One egg slightly has beaten
- 1/4 cup granulated

Directions

1. Place the milk, water, butter, egg sugar, salt, flour, and yeast in a pan.

2. Select dough setting and push start. Press the start button.

3. When the process is complete, remove dough from the pan and transfer it to a lightly floured surface.

4. Using a rolling pin lightly dusted with flour, roll dough to ½ inch thickness.

5. Cut with a floured dusted donut cutter or circle cookie cutter.

sugar

- 1 tsp salt
- 3 cups bread machine flour
- 2 1/2 tsp bread machine yeast
- oil for deep frying
- 1/4 cup confectioners' sugar

6. Transfer donuts to a baking sheet that has been covered with wax paper. Place another layer of paper on top, then cover with a clean tea towel. Let rise 30-40 minutes.

7. Heat vegetable oil to 375° (190°C°) in a deep-fryer or large, heavy pot.

8. Fry donuts 2-3 at a time until golden brown on both sides for about 3 minutes.

9. Drain on a paper towel.

10. Sprinkle with confectioners' sugar.

Nutrition Information

- Calories 180
- Carbohydrates: 30g
- Total Fat 5g
- Cholesterol 25mg
- Protein 4g
- Fiber 2g
- Sugar 7g
- Sodium 240mg
- Potassium 64mg

ORANGE BREAD

Servings: 1 loaf

Preparation time: **1 hour and 10 minutes**

Cook time: : **2 hour**

Ingredients

- 1 cup of orange juice
- One egg
- One tablespoon margarine
- ¼ cup hot water
- 3 1/2 cups bread flour
- ¼ cup white sugar
- Two tablespoons orange zest

Directions

1. Put all the ingredients in your bread pan according to the guidelines of the manufacturer.
2. Select the machine's basic or white bread cycle.
3. Press the start button.
4. Take out the pan when done and set aside for 10 minutes.

- One teaspoon salt
- One pack of active dry yeast

Nutrition Information

- Calories 210
- Carbohydrates: 45g
- Total Fat 3g
- Cholesterol 3mg
- Protein 5g
- Fiber 2g
- Sugar 15g
- Sodium 185mg
- Potassium 61mg

HAWAIIAN SWEET BREAD

Servings: 1 loaf

Preparation time: 1 hour and 10 minutes

Cook time: : 2 hour

Ingredients

- 3/4 cup pineapple juice
- One egg
- Two tablespoons vegetable oil
- 2 1/2 tablespoons honey
- 3/4 teaspoon salt
- 3 cups bread flour

Directions

1. Place ingredients in bread machine container.
2. Select the white bread cycle.
3. Press the start button.
4. Take out the pan when done and set aside for 10 minutes.

- Two tablespoons dry milk
- Two teaspoons fast-rising yeast

Nutrition Information

- Calories 169
- Carbohydrates: 25g
- Total Fat 5g
- Cholesterol 25mg
- Protein 4g
- Fiber 1g
- Sugar 5g
- Sodium 165mg
- Potassium 76mg

DATE AND NUT BREAD

Servings: 1 loaf

Preparation time: 1 hour and 10 minutes

Cook time: : 2 hour

Ingredients

- 1-1/2 tablespoons vegetable oil
- 1 cup of water
- ½ teaspoon salt
- Two tablespoons honey
- ¾ cup whole-wheat flour
- ¾ cup rolled oats
- 1 1/2 teaspoons

Directions

1. Put everything in your bread machine pan.
2. Select the primary cycle. Press the start button.
3. Take out the pan when done and set aside for 10 minutes.

active dry yeast

- 1 1/2 cups bread flour
- ½ cup almonds, chopped
- ½ cup dates, chopped and pitted

Nutrition Information

- Calories: 112 Cal
- Carbohydrates: 17 g
- Fat: 5g
- Cholesterol: 0 mg
- Protein: 3 g
- Fibre: 3 g
- Sugar: 7 g
- Sodium: 98 mg
- Potassium: 130 mg

Chapter 6: Perfect for Breakfast

BREAKFAST BREAD

Servings: 16 slices

Preparation time: **15 minutes**

Cook time: : **40 minutes**

Ingredients

- ½ tsp. Xanthan gum
- ½ tsp. salt
- 2 Tbsp. coconut oil
- ½ cup butter, melted
- 1 tsp. baking powder
- 2 cups of almond

Directions

1. Preheat the oven to 355F.
2. Beat eggs in a bowl on high for 2 minutes.
3. Add coconut oil and butter to the eggs and continue to beat.
4. Line a pan with baking paper and then pour the beaten eggs.

flour

- Seven eggs

5. Pour in the rest of the ingredients and mix until it becomes thick.

6. Bake until a toothpick comes out dry. It takes 40 to 45 minutes.

Nutrition Information

- Calories: 234
- Fat: 23g
- Carb: 1g
- Protein: 7g

PEANUT BUTTER AND JELLY BREAD

Servings: 1 loaf

Preparation time: 2 hours

Cook time: : 1 hour and 10 minutes

Ingredients

- 1 1/2 tablespoons vegetable oil
- 1 cup of water
- ½ cup blackberry jelly
- ½ cup peanut butter
- One teaspoon salt
- One tablespoon white sugar
- 2 cups of bread flour
- 1 cup whole-wheat

Directions

1. Put everything in your bread machine pan.
2. Select the basic setting.
3. Press the start button.
4. Take out the pan when done and set aside for 10 minutes.

flour

- 1 1/2 teaspoons
active dry yeast

Nutrition Information

- Calories: 153 Cal
- Carbohydrates: 20 g
- Fat: 9g
- Cholesterol: 0mg
- Protein: 4g
- Fiber: 2g
- Sugar: 11g
- Sodium: 244mg
- Potassium: 120mg

FINNISH PULLA

Servings: 1 loaf

Preparation time: 1 hour

Cook time: : 30 minutes

Ingredients

- 1 cup milk
- 1/4 cup water, lukewarm
- 3 eggs, 1 egg reserved for glaze
- 4 1/2 cups all purpose flour
- 1/2 cup sugar
- 1 teaspoon salt
- 1 tablespoon ground cardamom
- 1 tablespoon yeast

Directions

1. Place the milk, water, and 2 lightly beaten eggs in bread machine pan.

2. Add flour, sugar, salt, cardamom in the pan, then top it with yeast and butter. Program the bread machine to dough setting.

3. Remove the dough from the bread machine pan and place on a lightly floured surface. Divide the dough into 3 equal pieces. Roll each piece of dough into 10-14 inch strand and braid. Pinch and tuck the ends under and place on greased or parchment covered baking sheet. Lightly cover it with a clean kitchen towel and let it rise for about 30-45 minutes.

4. Preheat the oven to 325 degrees. Beat the remaining egg

- 1/4 cup butter, cut into 4 chunks
- 1-2 tablespoons pearl sugar for topping loaves

and gently brush the loaf on top and on the sides with pastry brush. Sprinkle with pearl sugar. Bake for 20 to 25 minutes until it becomes light golden brown. Cool on wire rack, then slice to serve.

Nutrition Information

- Total Fat 4.5g
- Saturated fat 2.5g
- Cholesterol 35mg
- Sodium 140mg
- Carbohydrates 26g
- Net carbs 25g
- Sugar 5g
- Fiber 1g
- Protein 4g

COFFEE BREAD

Ingredients

- 200 grams Bread flour
- 100 grams Cake flour
- 30 grams Sugar
- 20 grams Butter
- 25 grams Milk powder
- 1 tsp Yeast
- 1 1/2 tbsp Coffee powder
- 165 grams

Directions

1. Put all the liquid ingredients, followed by the dry ingredient. Leave the butter for later.

2. Press the dough function for it to spin 10 minutes. After that, add the butter and press basic/ sandwich function.

3. Take the bread out 10 minutes before its done.

4. Once done let it cool before cutting and serving.

Nutrition Information

- Saturated Fat 1.164 g
- Cholesterol 32mg
- Sodium 13mg
- Total Carbohydrate 49.54g
- Dietary Fiber 1.6g
- Sugars10.34g
- Protein6.46g

LOW-CARB BAGEL

Servings: 12 pcs

Preparation time: **15 minutes**

Cook time: : **25 minutes**

Ingredients

- 1 cup protein powder, unflavored
- 1/3 cup coconut flour
- 1 tsp. baking powder
- ½ tsp. sea salt
- ¼ cup ground flaxseed

Directions

1. Preheat the oven to 350F.
2. In a mixer, blend sour cream and eggs until well combined.
3. Whisk together the flaxseed, salt, baking powder, protein powder, and coconut flour in a bowl.
4. Mix the dry ingredients until it becomes wet ingredients. Make sure it is well blended.
5. Whisk the topping seasoning together in a small bowl. Set

119

- 1/3 cup sour cream
- 12 eggs
- Seasoning topping:
- 1 tsp. dried parsley
- 1 tsp. dried oregano
- 1 tsp. Dried minced onion
- ½ tsp. Garlic powder
- ½ tsp. Dried basil
- ½ tsp. sea salt

aside.

6. Grease 2 donut pans that can contain six donuts each.

7. Sprinkle pan with about 1 tsp. Topping seasoning and evenly pour batter into each.

8. Sprinkle the top of each bagel evenly with the rest of the seasoning mixture.

9. Bake in the oven for 25 minutes, or until golden brown.

Nutrition Information

- Calories: 134
- Fat: 6.8g
- Carb: 4.2g
- Protein: 12.1g

PURI BREAD

Servings: 6 pcs

Preparation time: **10 minutes**

Cook time: : **5 minutes**

Ingredients

- 1 cup almond flour, sifted
- ½ cup of warm water
- 2 Tbsp. clarified butter
- 1 cup olive oil for frying
- Salt to taste

Directions

1. Salt the water and add the flour.
2. Make some holes in the center of the dough and pour warm clarified butter.
3. Knead the dough and let stand for 15 minutes, covered.
4. Shape into six balls.
5. Flatten the balls into six thin rounds using a rolling pin.
6. Heat enough oil to cover a round frying pan completely.
7. Place a puri in it when hot.
8. Fry for 20 seconds on each side.

9. Place on a paper towel.

10. Repeat with the rest of the puri and serve.

Nutrition Information

- Calories: 106
- Fat: 3g
- Carb: 6g
- Protein: 3g

PITA BREAD WITH BLACK CUMIN

Servings: 8 pcs

Preparation time: **10 minutes**

Cook time: : **15 minutes**

Ingredients

- 2 cups almond flour, sifted
- ½ cup of water
- 2 Tbsp. olive oil
- Salt, to taste
- 1 tsp. black cumin

Directions

1. Preheat the oven to 400F.
2. Combine the flour with salt. Add the water and olive oil.
3. Knead the dough and let stand about 15 minutes.
4. Shape the dough into eight balls.
5. Line a baking sheet with parchment paper and flatten the balls into eight thin rounds.
6. Sprinkle black cumin.
7. Bake for 15 minutes, serve.

Nutrition Information

- Calories: 73
- Fat: 6.9g
- Carbohydrates: 1.6g
- Protein: 1.6g

BREAD ROLL

Servings: 8 pcs

Preparation time: **2 hours**

Cook time: : **50 minutes**

Ingredients

- 2 Tablespoons coconut oil, melted
- 6 Tablespoons coconut flour
- 1/4 teaspoon baking soda
- 1 Tablespoon Italian seasoning
- 1/2 teaspoon salt
- 2 Tablespoons gelatin

Directions

1. Preheat the oven to 300 F (150 C).
2. Mix the coconut oil, coconut flour, and baking soda.
3. In a separate bowl, whisk together the gelatin and hot water to create your gelatin egg.
4. Pour the gelatin egg into the coconut flour mixture and combine well.
5. Add in the Italian seasoning and salt to taste (you can taste the mixture to see if you want to add more) and mix well into a dough.
6. Use your hands to form 2 small rolls from the dough, place

- 6 Tablespoons hot water

the rolls on a baking tray lined with parchment paper, and bake in the oven for 40-50 minutes until the outside of each roll is slightly browned and crispy like you'd typically find in a regular bread roll.

7. Let the rolls cool down before serving so that the gelatin sets a bit and can hold the roll together. Enjoy at room temperature with some ghee or coconut oil.

8. This recipe can be doubled, tripled, etc. if you want to make more AIP bread rolls at the same time.

Nutrition Information

- Calories: 390,
- Fat: 23.6g
- Carbohydrates: 10.6g
- Protein: 33.5g

BACON BREAKFAST BAGELS

Servings: 3 pcs

Preparation time: **2 hours**

Cook time: : **50 minutes**

Ingredients

- Bagels
- ¾ cup (68 g) almond flour
- 1 teaspoon xanthan gum
- 1 large egg
- 1 ½ cups grated

Directions

1. Preheat oven to 390°F.

2. In a bowl mix together the almond flour and xanthan gum. Then add the egg and mix together until well combined. Set aside. It will look like a doughy ball.

3. In a pot over a medium-low heat slowly melt the cream cheese and mozzarella together and remove from heat once melted. This can be done in the microwave as well.

- mozzarella
- 2 tablespoons cream cheese
- Toppings
- 1 tablespoon butter, melted
- Sesame seeds to taste
- Fillings
- 2 tablespoons pesto
- 2 tablespoons cream cheese
- 1 cup arugula leaves
- 6 slices grilled streaky bacon

4. Add your melted cheese mix to the almond flour mix and knead until well combined. The Mozzarella mix will stick together in a bit of a ball but don't worry, persist with it. It will all combine well eventually. It's important to get the Xanthan gum incorporated through the cheese mix. Suppose the dough gets too tough to work, place in microwave for 10-20 seconds to warm and repeat until you have something that resembles a dough.

5. Split your dough into 3 pieces and roll into round logs. If you have a donut pan place your logs into the pan. If not, make circles with each log and join together and place on a baking tray. Try to make sure you have nice little circles. The other way to do this is to make a ball and flatten slightly on the baking tray and cut a circle out of the middle if you have a small cookie cutter.

6. Melt your butter and brush over the top of your bagels and sprinkle sesame seeds or your topping of choice. The butter should help the seeds stick. Garlic and onion powder or cheese make nice additions if you have them for savory bagels.

7. Place bagels in the oven for about 18 minutes. Keep an eye on them. The tops should go golden brown.

8. Take the bagels out of the oven and allow to cool.

9. If you like your bagels toasted, cut them in half lengthwise and place back in the oven until slightly golden and toasty.

10. Spread bagel with cream cheese, cover in pesto, add a few arugula leaves and top with your crispy bacon (or your filling of choice.)

Nutrition Information

- Calories: 605.67 Cal
- Fats: 50.29g
- Carbohydrates: 5.76g
- Protein: 30.13g

HOT DOG BUNS

Servings: 10 pcs

Preparation time: 10 minutes

Cook time: : 50 minutes

Ingredients

- One ¼ cups almond flour
- 5 tbsp. psyllium husk powder
- 1 tsp. sea salt
- 2 tsp. baking powder
- One ¼ cups boiling water
- 2 tsp. lemon juice
- Three egg whites

Directions

1. Preheat the oven to 350F
2. In a bowl, put all dry ingredients and mix well.
3. Add boiling water, lemon juice, and egg whites into the dry mixture and whisk until combined.
4. Mould the dough into ten portions and roll into buns.
5. Transfer into the preheated oven and cook for 40 to 50 minutes on the lower oven rack.
6. Check for doneness and remove it.
7. Top with desired toppings and hot dogs and serve.

Nutrition Information

- Calories: 104
- Fat: 8g
- Carb: 1g
- Protein: 4g

PALEO COCONUT BREAD

Servings: **10 pcs**

Preparation time: **10 minutes**

Cook time: : **50 minutes**

Ingredients

- ½ cup coconut flour
- ¼ cup almond milk (unsweetened)
- ¼ cup coconut oil (melted)
- 6 eggs
- ¼ tsp. baking soda
- ¼ tsp. salt

Directions

1. Preheat the oven to 350F.
2. Prepare a (8 x 4) bread pan with parchment paper.
3. In a bowl, combine salt, baking soda, and coconut flour.
4. Combine the oil, milk, and eggs in another bowl.
5. Gradually add the wet ingredients into the dry ingredients and mix well.
6. Pour the mixture into the prepared pan.
7. Bake for 40 to 50 minutes.
8. Cool, slice, and serve.

Nutrition Information

- Calories: 108
- Fat: 8.7g
- Carb: 3.4g
- Protein: 4.2g

HEALTHY LOW CARB BREAD

Servings: 8 slices

Preparation time: 15 minutes

Cook time: : 35 minutes

Ingredients

- 2/3 cup coconut flour
- 2/3 cup coconut oil (softened not melted)
- Nine eggs
- 2 tsp. Cream of tartar
- ¾ tsp. xanthan gum
- 1 tsp. Baking soda
- ¼ tsp. salt
-

Directions

1. Preheat the oven to 350F.
2. Grease a loaf pan with 1 to 2 tsp. Melted coconut oil and place it in the freezer to harden.
3. Add eggs into a bowl and mix for 2 minutes with a hand mixer.
4. Add coconut oil into the eggs and mix.
5. Add dry ingredients to a second bowl and whisk until mixed.
6. Put the dry ingredients into the egg mixture and mix on low speed with a hand mixer until dough is formed and

the mixture is incorporated.

7. Add the dough into the prepared loaf pan, transfer into the preheated oven, and bake for 35 minutes.

8. Take out the bread pan from the oven.

9. Cool, slice, and serve.

Nutrition Information

- Calories: 229
- Fat: 25.5g Carb: 6.5g
- Protein: 8.5g

SPICY BREAD

Servings: 6 pcs

Preparation time: **10 minutes**

Cook time: : **40 minutes**

Ingredients

- ½ cup coconut flour
- Six eggs
- Three large jalapenos, sliced
- 4 ounces' turkey bacon, sliced
- ½ cup ghee
- ¼ tsp. baking soda

Directions

1. Preheat the oven to 400F.
2. Cut bacon and jalapenos on a baking tray and roast for 10 minutes.
3. Flip and bake for five more minutes.
4. Remove seeds from the jalapenos.
5. Place jalapenos and bacon slices in a food processor and blend until smooth.
6. In a bowl, add ghee, eggs, and ¼-cup water. Mix well.

- ¼ tsp. salt
- ¼ cup of water

7. Then add some coconut flour, baking soda, and salt. Stir to mix.
8. Add bacon and jalapeno mix.
9. Grease the loaf pan with ghee.
10. Pour batter into the loaf pan.
11. Bake for 40 minutes.
12. Enjoy.

Nutrition Information

- Calories: 240
- Fat: 20g

FLUFFY PALEO BREAD

Servings: **15 slices**

Preparation time: **10 minutes**

Cook time: : **40 minutes**

Ingredients

- One ¼ cup almond flour
- Five eggs
- 1 tsp. lemon juice
- 1/3 cup avocado oil
- One dash black pepper
- ½ tsp. sea salt
- 3 to 4 tbsp. tapioca

Directions

1. Preheat the oven to 350F.
2. Line a baking pan with parchment paper and set aside.
3. In a bowl, add eggs, avocado oil, and lemon juice and whisk until combined.
4. In another bowl, add tapioca flour, almond flour, baking soda, flaxseed, black pepper, and poppy seed. Mix.
5. Add the lemon juice mixture into the flour mixture and mix well.
6. Add the batter into the prepared loaf pan and top with

flour

- 1 to 2 tsp. Poppyseed
- ¼ cup ground flaxseed
- ½ tsp. baking soda
- Top with:
- Poppy seeds
- Pumpkin seeds

extra pumpkin seeds and poppy seeds.

7. Cover loaf pan and transfer into the prepared oven, and bake for 20 minutes. Remove cover and bake until an inserted knife comes out clean after about 15 to 20 minutes.

8. Remove from oven and cool.

9. Slice and serve.

Nutrition Information

- Calories: 149 Cal
- Fat: 12.9 g
- Carbohydrates: 4.4 g

Chapter 7: International bread

GERMAN PUMPERNICKEL BREAD

Servings: 1 loaf

Preparation time: **2 hours**

Cook time: : **1 hour and 10 minutes**

Ingredients

- 1 1/2 tablespoon vegetable oil
- 1 1/8 cups warm water
- Three tablespoons cocoa
- 1/3 cup molasses
- 1 ½ teaspoons salt

Directions

1. Put everything in your bread machine.
2. Select the primary cycle.
3. Hit the start button.
4. Transfer bread to a rack for cooling once done.

- One tablespoon caraway seeds
- 1 cup rye flour
- 1 ½ cups of bread flour
- 1 ½ tablespoon wheat gluten
- 1 cup whole wheat flour
- 2 ½ teaspoons bread machine yeast

Nutrition Information

- Calories 119
- Carbohydrates: 22.4 g
- Total Fat 2.3 g
- Cholesterol 0mg
- Protein 3 g
- Sodium 295 mg

EUROPEAN BLACK BREAD

Servings: 1 loaf

Preparation time: **2 hours**

Cook time: : **1 hour and 5 minutes**

Ingredients

- ¾ teaspoon cider vinegar
- 1 cup of water
- ½ cup rye flour
- 1 ½ cups flour
- One tablespoon margarine
- ¼ cup of oat bran
- One teaspoon salt
- 1 ½ tablespoons sugar
- One teaspoon dried onion flakes

Directions

1. Put everything in your bread machine.
2. Now select the basic setting.
3. Hit the start button.
4. Transfer bread to a rack for cooling once done.

- One teaspoon caraway seed
- One teaspoon yeast
- Two tablespoons unsweetened cocoa

Nutrition Information

- Calories 114
- Carbohydrates: 22 g
- Total Fat 1.7 g
- Cholesterol 0mg
- Protein 3 g
- Sugar 2 g
- Sodium 247 mg

FRENCH BAGUETTES

Servings: 2 loaves

Preparation time: **25 minutes**

Cook time: : **15 minutes**

Ingredients

- One ¼ cups warm water
- 3 ½ cups bread flour
- One teaspoon salt
- One package active dry yeast

Directions

1. Place ingredients in the bread machine. Select the dough cycle. Hit the start button.
2. When the dough cycle is finished, remove it with floured hands and cut in half on a well-floured.
3. Take each half of dough and roll it to make a loaf about 12 inches long in the shape of French bread.
4. Place on a greased baking sheet and cover with a towel.
5. Let rise until doubled, about 1 hour.
6. Preheat oven to 450 F (220 ° C).
7. Bake until golden brown, turning the pan around once

halfway during baking.

8. Transfer the loaves to a rack.

Nutrition Information

- Calories 201
- Carbohydrates: 42 g
- Total Fat 0.6 g
- Cholesterol 0 mg
- Protein 6 g
- Fiber 1.7 g
- Sugar 0.1 g
- Sodium 293 mg

ITALIAN BREAD

Servings: 2 loaves

Preparation time: **2 hours**

Cook time: : **1 hour and 10 minutes**

Ingredients

- One tablespoon of light brown sugar
- 4 cups all-purpose flour, unbleached
- 1 ½ teaspoon of salt
- One 1/3 cups + 1 tablespoon warm water
- One package active dry yeast

Directions

1. Place flour, brown sugar, 1/3 cup warm water, salt, olive oil, and yeast in your bread machine. Select the dough cycle. Hit the start button.
2. Deflate your dough. Turn it on a floured surface.
3. Form two loaves from the dough.
4. Keep them on your cutting board. The seam side should be down. Sprinkle some cornmeal on your board.
5. Place a damp cloth on your loaves to cover them.
6. Wait for 40 minutes. The volume should double.

- 1 ½ teaspoon of olive oil
- One egg
- Two tablespoons cornmeal

7. In the meantime, preheat your oven to 190 °C.
8. Beat 1 tablespoon of water and an egg in a bowl.
9. Brush this mixture on your loaves.
10. Make an extended cut at the center of your loaves with a knife.
11. Shake your cutting board gently, making sure that the loaves do not stick.
12. Now slide your loaves on a baking sheet.
13. Bake in your oven for about 35 minutes.

Nutrition Information

- Calories 105
- Carbohydrates: 20.6 g
- Total Fat 0.9 g
- Cholesterol 9 mg
- Protein 3.1 g
- Fiber 1 g
- Sugar 1g
- Sodium 179 mg
- Potassium 39 mg

PORTUGUESE SWEET BREAD

Servings: 1 loaf

Preparation time: 2 hours

Cook time: : 1 hour and 5 minutes

Ingredients

- One egg beaten
- 1 cup milk
- 1/3 cup sugar
- Two tablespoons margarine
- 3 cups bread flour
- ¾ teaspoon salt
- 2 ½ teaspoons active dry yeast

Directions

1. Place everything into your bread machine.
2. Select the sweet bread setting. Hit the start button.
3. Transfer the loaves to a rack for cooling once done.

Nutrition Information

- Calories 139
- Carbohydrates: 24 g
- Total Fat 8.3 g
- Cholesterol 14 mg
- Protein 3 g
- Fiber 0g
- Sugar 4 g
- Sodium 147 mg

PITA BREAD

Servings: 8 pcs

Preparation time: 35 minutes

Cook time: : 20 minutes

Ingredients

- 3 cups of all-purpose flour
- 1 1/8 cups warm water
- One tablespoon of vegetable oil
- One teaspoon salt
- 1 ½ teaspoon active dry yeast
- One active teaspoon

Directions

1. Place all the ingredients in your bread pan.
2. Select the dough setting. Hit the start button.
3. The machine beeps after the dough rises adequately.
4. Turn the dough on a floured surface.
5. Roll and stretch the dough gently into a 12-inch rope.
6. Cut into eight pieces with a knife.
7. Now roll each piece into a ball. It should be smooth.
8. Roll each ball into a 7-inch circle. Keep covered with a towel on a floured top for 30 minutes for the pita to rise. It

white sugar

should get puffy slightly.

9. Preheat your oven to 260 degrees C.

10. Keep the pitas on your wire cake rack. Transfer to the oven rack directly.

11. Bake the pitas for 5 minutes. They should be puffed. The top should start to brown.

12. Take out from the oven. Keep the pitas immediately in a sealed paper bag. You can also cover using a damp kitchen towel.

13. Split the top edge or cut into half once the pitas are soft. You can also have the whole pitas if you want.

Nutrition Information

- Calories 191
- Carbohydrates: 37g
- Total Fat 3g
- Cholesterol 0mg
- Protein 5g
- Fiber 1g
- Sugar 1g
- Sodium 293mg
- Potassium 66mg

SYRIAN BREAD

Servings: 8 pcs

Preparation time: **20 minutes**

Cook time: : **20 minutes**

Ingredients

- Two tablespoons vegetable oil
- 1 cup of water
- 1 ½ teaspoons salt
- ½ teaspoon white sugar
- 1 ½ teaspoon active dry yeast
- 3 cups all-purpose flour

Directions

1. Put everything in your bread machine pan.
2. Select the dough cycle. Hit the start button.
3. Preheat your oven to 475 degrees F.
4. Turn to dough on a lightly floured surface once done.
5. Divide it into eight equal pieces. Form them into rounds.
6. Take a damp cloth and cover the rounds with it.
7. Now roll the dough into flat thin circles. They should have a diameter of around 8 inches.
8. Cook in your preheated baking sheets until they are

Nutrition Information

- Calories 204
- Carbohydrates: 36g
- Total Fat 5g
- Cholesterol 0mg
- Protein 5g
- Fiber 1g
- Sugar 0g
- Sodium 438mg
- Potassium 66mg

SOUR CREAM CHIEVE BREAD

Servings: 1 loaf

Preparation time: **10 minutes**

Cook time: : **3 hours**

Ingredients

- 2/3 cup whole milk (70° to 80°)
- 1/4 cup water (70° to 80°)
- 1/4 cup sour cream
- 2 tablespoons butter
- 1-1/2 teaspoons sugar
- 1-1/2 teaspoons salt
- 3 cups bread flour

Directions

1. Place all the ingredients in the bread machine pan, in the order suggested by the manufacturer.
2. Select basic bread setting.
3. Choose crust coolor and loaf size if available.
4. Bake according to bread machine directions
5. Check the dough after 5 minutes of mixing and add 1 or 2 tablespoons of water or flour if needed.

- 1/8 teaspoon baking soda
- 1/4 cup minced chives
- 2-1/4 teaspoons active dry yeast

Nutrition Information

- Calories 105
- Fat 2g
- Saturated fat 2g
- Cholesterol 8mg
- Sodium 253mg
- Carbohydrate 18g
- Protein 4g

SWEDISH CARDAMOM BREAD

Servings: 1 loaf

Preparation time: 35 minutes

Cook time: : 15 minutes

Ingredients

- ¼ cup of sugar
- ¾ cup of warm milk
- ¾ teaspoon cardamom
- ½ teaspoon salt
- ¼ cup of softened butter
- One egg
- Two ¼ teaspoons bread machine yeast

Directions

1. Put everything (except milk for brushing and sugar for sprinkling) in the pan of your bread machine.

2. Select the dough cycle. Hit the start button. You should have an elastic and smooth dough once the process is complete. It should be double in size.

3. Transfer to a lightly floured surface.

4. Now divide into three balls. Set aside for 10 minutes.

5. Roll all the balls into long ropes of around 14 inches.

6. Braid the shapes. Pinch ends under securely and keeps on a cookie sheet. You can also divide your dough into two

- 3 cups all-purpose flour
- Five tablespoons milk for brushing
- Two tablespoons sugar for sprinkling

balls. Smooth them and keep on your bread pan.

7. Brush milk over the braid. Sprinkle sugar lightly.
8. Now bake in your oven for 25 minutes at 375 degrees F (190 degrees C).
9. Take a foil and cover for the final 10 minutes. It's prevents over-browning.
10. Transfer to your cooling rack.

Nutrition Information

- Calories 135
- Carbohydrates: 22g
- Total Fat 7g
- Cholesterol 20mg
- Protein 3g
- Fiber 1g
- Sugar 3g
- Sodium 100mg

ETHIOPIAN MILK AND HONEY BREAD

Servings: 1 loaf

Preparation time: 2 hours

Cook time: : 1 hour and 15 minutes

Ingredients

- Three tablespoons honey
- 1 cup + 1 tablespoon milk
- 3 cups bread flour
- Three tablespoons melted butter
- Two teaspoons active dry yeast
- 1 ½ teaspoons salt

Directions

1. Add everything to the pan of your bread
2. Select the white bread or basic setting and the medium crust setting.
3. Hit the start button.
4. Take out your hot loaf once it is done.
5. Keep on your wire rack for cooling.
6. Slice your bread once it is cold and serve.

Nutrition Information

- Calories 129
- Carbohydrates: 20 g
- Total Fat 3.8 g
- Cholesterol 0 mg
- Protein 2.4 g
- Fiber 0.6 g
- Sugars 3.3 g
- Sodium 78 mg

FIJI SWEET POTATO BREAD

Servings: 1 loaf

Preparation time: **2 hours**

Cook time: : **1 hour and 10minutes**

Ingredients

- One teaspoon vanilla extract
- ½ cup of warm water
- 4 cups flour
- 1 cup sweet mashed potatoes
- Two tablespoons softened butter
- ½ teaspoon cinnamon
- 1 ½ teaspoons salt
- 1/3 cup brown sugar

Directions

1. Add everything in the pan of your bread.
2. Select the white bread and the crust you want.
3. Hit the start button.
4. Set aside on wire racks for cooling before slicing.

- Two tablespoons powdered milk
- Two teaspoons yeast

Nutrition Information

- Calories: 168 Cal
- Carbohydrates: 28 g
- Fat: 5g
- Cholesterol: 0 mg
- Protein: 4 g
- Fiber: 1g
- Sugat 3 g
- Sodium: 292 mg

Chapter 8: Desserts and Cookies

CHOCOLATE CHIP BREAD

Servings: 15 pcs

Preparation time: 5 minutes

Cook time: 2 hours and 55 minutes

Ingredients

- 1 1/3 Cups – Milk (lukewarm)
- 4 Tablespoons – Butter
- 4 Cups – Bread Flour
- 1/3 Cup – Brown Sugar

Directions

1. Bread Machine settings – 2 pound loaf, light color and "basic" bread setting

2. Add all of the ingredients (except the chocolate chips) starting with the milk into the bread machine pan.

3. 1 or 2 minutes after starting your bread machine (during the first kneading/mixing cycle), add 50% of the chocolate chips. Let the milk & flour be fully mixed before adding

- 1 1/2 Teaspoons – Salt
- 1 1/2 Teaspoons – Bread Machine Yeast
- 3/4 Cup – Semi-Sweet Chocolate Chips

the other chips.

4. Place the chocolate chips that are left in the bread container after the first kneading cycle is complete (around the 10 minute mark in our Sunbeam machine) and before the second/final kneading cycle starts.

5. When the bread machine has finished baking the bread, remove the bread and place it on a cooling rack.

Nutrition Information

- Calories: 290 Cal
- Carbohydrates: 28 g
- Fat: 5g

PORTUGESE SWEET BREAD

Servings: 1 loaf

Preparation time: 5 minutes

Cook time: : 3 hours

Ingredients

- 1 cup milk
- 1 egg
- 2 tablespoons margarine
- ⅓ cup white sugar
- ¾ teaspoon salt
- 3 cups bread flour
- 2 ½ teaspoons active dry yeast

Directions

1. Add ingredients in order suggested by your manufacturer.
2. Select "sweet bread" setting.

Nutrition Information

- Calories 56
- Protein 1.5g
- Carbohydrates 6.9g
- Fat: 2.6g

WHITE CHOCOLATE BREAD

Servings: 1 loaf

Preparation time: 5 minutes

Cook time: : 2 hours and 55 minutes

Ingredients

- ¼ cup warm water
- 1 cup warm milk
- 1 egg
- ¼ cup butter, softened
- 3 cups bread flour
- 2 tablespoons brown sugar
- 2 tablespoons white sugar

Directions

1. Place all ingredients (except the white chocolate chips) in the pan of the bread machine in the order recommended by the manufacturer.

2. Select cycle; press Start.

3. If your machine has a Fruit setting, add the white chocolate chips at the signal, otherwise you can do it about 5 minutes before the kneading cycle has finished.

- 1 teaspoon salt
- 1 teaspoon ground cinnamon
- 1 (.25 ounce) package active dry yeast
- 1 cup white chocolate chips

Nutrition Information

- Calories 277
- Protein 6.6g
- Carbohydrates 39g
- Fat: 10.5g

BRIOSCHES

Servings: 1 loaf

Preparation time: **10 minutes**

Cook time: : **1 hour and 20 minutes**

Ingredients

- 1/4 cup milk
- 2 tablespoons water
- 1 tablespoon extra virgin olive oil
- 3 tablespoons honey
- 2 whole eggs
- 1 egg yolk
- 2 cups all-purpose flour

Directions

1. Add the first six ingredients into the pail of your bread machine.

2. Mix the flour and the salt in a bowl; then add it to the wet ingredients.

3. Make a small well in the flour, then add the yeast.

4. Choose the "sweet" setting in your bread machine and choose se "light crust" option. Start the machine.

5. After around 30 seconds, drop the 7 tablespoons of butter, one by one. It is important to give time to each tablespoon of butter to get incorporated with the flour

- 3/4 teaspoon Himalayan salt
- 1 3/4 teaspoons active dry yeast
- 7 tablespoons butter

mixture.

6. Let the bread bake.

7. When done, leave the bread in the machine for about 15 to 20 minutes with the lid open.

8. Remove the bread from the pail and enjoy!

Nutrition Information

- Calories 219
- Protein 6.6g
- Carbohydrates 32g
- Fat: 10.5g

CINNAMON BABAKA

Servings: 1 loaf

Preparation time: **3 hours**

Cook time: : **45 minutes**

Ingredients

- For the Dough
- ¾ c milk, warmed to 80-90F
- 2 ¼ tsp (1 packet) active dry yeast
- 4 Tbsp unsalted butter
- 3 Tbsp sugar

Directions

FOR THE DOUGH:

1. In a small bowl, mix the warmed milk and yeast. Let this mixture to rest aside for 5-10 minutes, until the yeast starts to foam.

2. Meanwhile, cream the butter and sugar together with an electric hand mixer in a medium bowl. Add, one at a time, the egg yolks, while beating them. Set this mixture aside too.

- 2 egg yolks (reserve the whites, separately, see below)
- 1 tsp pure vanilla extract
- 2 eggs (whole)
- 3 ½ - 4 c unbleached all-purpose flour
- 1 tsp salt
- For the Filling
- 1 c brown sugar
- 1 Tbsp cinnamon
- ¼ tsp salt
- 2 Tbsp unsalted butter melted and cooled
- 1 egg white (see above)
- For the Egg Wash
- 1 egg white (see above), lightly beaten

3. Give the yeast mixture a stir, then add it to the bowl of your bread machine. Add the egg and butter mixture to the milk.

4. Pour the salt and 3 cups of flour..

5. Start your bread machine on its Dough Cycle. Watch your dough as it begins to knead. Once it looks like the ingredients are completely mixed, add more flour, a ¼ cup at a time, letting the machine knead between each addition, until the dough comes together and pulls away from the sides of the bowl.

6. When it happens, close your bread machine and let the machine run through its Dough Cycle. When the cycle is done, wait for the bread to become double its size.

7. FOR THE FILLING:

8. Now make the filling by whisking all of the filling ingredients together in a medium bowl, until it becomes smooth and then let it set aside.

9. PUTTING IT ALL TOGETHER

10. Grease a 9x5 loaf pan and line it with greased parchment paper.

11. Tip the dough out of its rising bowl onto a well-floured surface.

12. Punch the dough down and roll it out into a roughly 18x15 inch rectangle.

13. Spread filling evenly over dough, leaving a 1 inch border on the long sides.

14. Roll the dough, starting from one of the long sides.

15. Cut the roll in half, lengthwise, turning it into two strands.

16. Twist the two strands together, trying to keep the cut (exposed filling) side on top, as much as possible.

17. Finally, shape your twisted dough into a figure 8, again keeping the cut sides up as much as possible. Place this twisted figure 8 into the greased and lined loaf pan.

18. Cover the dough in the pan loosely with plastic wrap and let rise for 30 minutes.

19. After 30 minutes, preheat your oven to 350F.

20. When the dough has risen slightly and looks puffy, remove the plastic wrap and brush the top of the dough

with the beaten egg white egg wash.

21. Bake the bread at 350F for 45-55 minutes, until the top crust is deeply golden and the loaf sounds hollow when tapped. (The internal temperature of the loaf should read around 180F when the bread is done). (It may be helpful to place a piece of aluminum foil or an aluminum foil lined baking sheet on the rack under the bread to catch any filling that my bubble out of the loaf.)

22. Once the loaf is done, cool the bread in the pan for 10 minutes, before gently removing the bread from the pan to continue to cool for 10-20 minutes before slicing.

23. The babka will stay fresh stored in airtight container at room temperature for up to 3 days, then move the bread to the refrigerator.

Nutrition Information

- Calories 219
- Protein 6.6g
- Carbohydrates 32g
- Fat: 10.5g

SOFT PRETZELS

Servings: 24 pcs

Preparation time: **10 minutes**

Cook time: : **20 minutes**

Ingredients

- oz. cocoa butter
- ½ cup coconut butter
- ½ cup sugar-free maple syrup
- 1/3 cup heavy cream

Directions

1. Start by throwing all the ingredients into a saucepan.
2. Stir cook on low heat until butter is melted, then stir well.
3. Spread this mixture in an 8x8-inch pan lined with parchment paper.
4. Refrigerate for 3 hours, then slice into 24 pieces.

- 3 tbsp coconut oil
- Two scoops matcha MCT powder
- 2 tsp vanilla essence

Nutrition Information

- Calories 173
- Total Fat 13 g
- Saturated Fat 10.1 g
- Cholesterol 12 mg
- Sodium 67 mg
- Total Carbs 7.5 g
- Sugar 1.2 g
- Fibre 0.6 g
- Protein 3.2 g

NO-BAKE BUTTER COOKIES

Servings: 8 pcs

Preparation time: **1 hour and 10 minutes**

Cook time: : **0 minutes**

Ingredients

- ½ cup almond flour
- 1½ tbsp butter
- 1 tbsp Swerve
- ½ tsp vanilla extract
- 1 pinch salt

Directions

1. Mix all the ingredients in a bowl to prepare the cookie batter.
2. Spoon out the batter onto a cookie sheet positioned on a baking tray.
3. Put the tray in the refrigerator and refrigerate for about 1 hour 10 minutes.
4. Serve the cookies.

Nutrition Information

- Calories: 125 Cal

- Fat: 3.2 g
- Cholesterol: 11 mg
- Sodium: 75 mg
- Carbohydrates: 3,6 g

CINNAMON BUTTER COOKIES

Servings: 12 pcs

Preparation time: 10 minutes

Cook time: : 12 minutes

Ingredients

- 2 cups Almond Flour
- ¼ tsp Salt
- ½ tsp Cinnamon Powder
- One stick butter softened
- 1 tsp Vanilla Extract
- ½ cup Swerve

Directions

1. Preheat oven to 350F.
2. Put Whisk together the almond flour, salt, cinnamon, and sweetener in a bowl.
3. Cut in the butter until the mixture resembles a coarse meal.
4. Mix in the egg and vanilla extract.
5. Scoop the dough into a baking sheet lined with parchment. Press slightly to flatten.

Granular Sweetener

- 1 Whole Egg

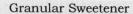

6. Bake for 12 minutes.

Nutrition Information

- Kcal per serve: 171
- Fat: 16 g. (82%)
- Protein: 4 g. (9%)
- Carbs: 3 g. (9%)

PEANUT BUTTER COOKIES

Servings: 12 pcs

Preparation time: **10 minutes**

Cook time: : **12 minutes**

Ingredients

- 1 cup Peanut Butter(sugar-free)
- ½ cup Erythritol
- 1 Whole Egg

Directions

1. Mix all ingredients into a bowl until it is combined.
2. Scoop the dough into a baking sheet lined with parchment. Press slightly to flatten.
3. Bake for 12 minutes.

Nutrition Information

- Kcal per serve: 136
- Fat: 12 g.
- Protein: 5 g.
- Carbs: 2g.

MATCHA COCONUT COOKIES

Servings: 12 pcs

Preparation time: 10 minutes

Cook time: : 12 minutes

Ingredients

- 1/3 cup Almond Flour
- 1/3 cup Coconut Flour
- 2 tbsp Matcha Powder
- ½ cup Swerve Granular Sweetener
- ½ tsp Baking Powder
- ½ cup Coconut Oil

Directions

1. Put Whisk together almond flour, coconut flour, sweetener, matcha, and baking powder in a bowl.
2. Add in the egg and coconut oil. Mix until well combined.
3. Scoop the dough into a baking sheet lined with parchment. Press slightly to flatten.
4. Bake for 12 minutes.

- 1 Whole Egg

Nutrition Information

- Kcal per serve: 112
- Fat: 12 g. (91%)
- Protein: 2 g. (5%)
- Carbs: 1 g. (4%)

ALMOND BANANA PANCAKES

Servings: 4 pcs

Preparation time: **10 minutes**

Cook time: : **10 minutes**

Ingredients

- 1 Ripe Banana, mashed
- 4 Eggs
- 1/2 cup Almond Flour
- 2 tbsp Erythritol
- 1 tsp Baking Powder
- 1 tsp Ground Cinnamon

Directions

1. Whisk together almond flour, baking powder, and cinnamon in a bowl.
2. In a separate bowl, mix mashed banana, eggs, and erythritol.
3. Gradually fold in the dry ingredients until becoming a wet mixture.
4. Preheat a skillet and coat with non-stick spray.
5. Spoon in the batter and cook for 1-2 minutes per side.

Nutrition Information

- Kcal per serve: 235
- Fat: 17 g. (64%)
- Protein: 11 g. (21%)
- Carbs: 10 g. (16%)

Chapter 9: Keto Bread

ZESTY POPPY SEED BREAD

Servings: 1 loaf

Preparation time: **15 minutes**

Cook time: : **1 hour and 30 minutes**

Ingredients

- 9.5 ounces almond flour
- Two lemons, zest only
- ½ cup no-calorie sweetener of your choice
- Three tablespoons

Directions

1. Put the wet ingredients, followed by the dry ingredients, into the bread pan.
2. Select the "Quick" or "Cake" mode of your bread machine.
3. Allow the cycles to be completed.
4. Remove the bread pan from the machine but keep the bread in the container for another 10 minutes.
5. Take out the bread from the bread pan, and let it cool

butter

down completely before slicing.

- Two tablespoons poppy seeds
- ½ teaspoon baking powder
- Six eggs
- Two tablespoons lemon juice
- Two tablespoons water

Nutrition Information

- Calories: 70
- Carbohydrates: 6g
- Fat: 17g
- Protein: 9g

SWEET CHALLA

Servings: 1 loaf

Preparation time: **3 hours**

Cook time: : **45 minutes**

Ingredients

- 1 ½ cup cream cheese
- 1 cup protein powder, unflavored and unsweetened
- 2/3 cup protein powder, vanilla flavour and unsweetened
- 1/3 cup no-calorie

Directions

1. Set aside two tablespoons of the beaten eggs for later use.
2. Put the wet ingredients first, then the dry ingredients into the bread pan.
3. Press the "Manual" or "Dough" setting on the bread machine.
4. Once completed, transfer the dough to a surface that has been lightly dusted with almond flour.
5. Remove the air bubbles by punching the dough.

- sweetener of your choice
- ¼ cup dried cranberries
- ¼ cup butter
- ¼ cup almond flour
- 2 ½ teaspoons baking powder
- One teaspoon xanthan gum
- ½ teaspoon salt
- 1/3 teaspoon salt
- Four eggs, beaten
- ¼ cup heavy cream
- ¼ cup oil

6. Divide the dough into 3.
7. Roll each piece until it becomes 16 inches long.
8. Braid the three pieces together on a lightly greased baking sheet.
9. Allow the dough to rise for about 30 minutes while preheating the oven to 4000F.
10. Brush the dough on the top with the reserved eggs from earlier.
11. Bake for 45 minutes, or until it is golden brown.

Nutrition Information

- Calories: 158
- Carbohydrates: 2g
- Fat: 13g
- Protein: 9g

LOW-CARB APPLE BREAD

Servings: 1 loaf

Preparation time: **20 minutes**

Cook time: : **1 hour and 30 minutes**

Ingredients

- Two apples, peeled and chopped
- 2 cups almond flour
- ½ cup golden flaxseed, milled
- ½ cup no-calorie sweetener of your choice
- Two teaspoons cinnamon

Directions

1. Place all ingredients in the pan according to the order specified above.
2. Set the bread machine to "Cake" or "Quick" mode.
3. Let the cycles finish.
4. Remove the bread pan from the machine, but keep the bread in the pan for another 10 minutes.
5. Slice the bread only when it has cooled down.

- ¾ teaspoon baking soda
- ¾ teaspoon salt
- ½ teaspoon nutmeg
- Four eggs, lightly beaten
- ¼ cup of water
- ¼ cup heavy cream
- Four tablespoons coconut oil
- Two teaspoons vanilla extract
- 1 ½ teaspoon apple cider vinegar

Nutrition Information

- Calories: 242
- Carbohydrates: 11g
- Fat: 20g
- Protein: 7g

KETO PUMPKIN BREAD

Servings: 1 loaf

Preparation time: **15 minutes**

Cook time: : **1 hour and 30 minutes**

Ingredients

- 1 ½ cup almond flour
- ½ cup coconut flour
- 2/3 cup no-calorie sweetener of your choice
- ½ cup butter softened
- One teaspoon cinnamon
- ½ teaspoon nutmeg

Directions

1. Add the wet ingredients followed by dry ingredients into the bread pan.
2. Use the "Quick" or "Cake" mode of the bread machine.
3. Wait until the cycles are done.
4. Remove the pan from the machine, but take out the bread from the pan for 10 mins.
5. Let the bread cool down first before slicing it completely.

- ½ teaspoon salt
- ¼ teaspoon ginger, grated
- 1/8 teaspoon ground cloves
- Four eggs
- ¾ cup pumpkin puree
- Four teaspoons baking powder
- One teaspoon vanilla extract

Nutrition Information

- Calories: 242
- Carbohydrates: 11g
- Fat: 20g
- Protein: 7g

LOW-CARB SODA BREAD

Servings: 1 loaf

Preparation time: **10 minutes**

Cook time: : **1 hour and 30 minutes**

Ingredients

- 2 cups almond flour
- ½ cup coconut flour
- ½ cup no-calorie sweetener of your choice
- ¼ cup raisins, chopped
- Three tablespoons butter softened
- Two teaspoons baking

Directions

1. Add all the ingredients to the pan in the following order: buttermilk, eggs, sweetener, salt, baking soda, baking powder, flour, butter, and raisins.
2. Use the "Quick" or "Cake" setting of the bread machine.
3. Wait until all cycles are finished.
4. Remove the pan from the machine.
5. Wait for another 10 minutes before taking out the bread from the pan.
6. Slice only when the bread has completely cooled down.

powder

- ½ teaspoon baking soda
- ¼ teaspoon salt
- Two eggs
- 1 cup buttermilk

Nutrition Information

- Calories: 113
- Carbohydrates: 6g
- Fat: 6g
- Protein: 4g

LOW-CARB SODA BREAD

Servings: 1 loaf

Preparation time: **10 minutes**

Cook time: : **1 hour and 30 minutes**

Ingredients

- 2 cups almond flour
- ½ cup coconut flour
- ½ cup no-calorie sweetener of your choice
- ¼ cup raisins, chopped
- Three tablespoons butter softened
- Two teaspoons baking

Directions

1. Add all the ingredients to the pan in the following order: buttermilk, eggs, sweetener, salt, baking soda, baking powder, flour, butter, and raisins.
2. Use the "Quick" or "Cake" setting of the bread machine.
3. Wait until all cycles are finished.
4. Remove the pan from the machine.
5. Wait for another 10 minutes before taking out the bread from the pan.
6. Slice only when the bread has completely cooled down.

powder

- ½ teaspoon baking soda
- ¼ teaspoon salt
- Two eggs
- 1 cup buttermilk

Nutrition Information

- Calories: 113
- Carbohydrates: 6g
- Fat: 6g
- Protein: 4g

KETO COCONUT BREAD

Ingredients

- ½ cup coconut flour
- ½ cup ground flaxseed
- Two tablespoons no-calorie sweetener of your choice
- One tablespoon baking powder

Directions

1. Put all the wet ingredients first into the bread pan before adding the dry ingredients.
2. Press the "Quick" or "Cake" setting of your bread machine.
3. Remove the pan from the machine once all cycles are finished.
4. Keep the bread in the pan for ten more minutes.
5. Take out the bread on the pan and let it cool down.

- One teaspoon xanthan gum
- ½ teaspoon ground cinnamon
- ½ teaspoon salt
- Six eggs
- 1/3 cup coconut milk
- 1/3 cup coconut oil

6. Slice and serve.

Nutrition Information

- Calories: 122
- Carbohydrates: 4g
- Fat: 9g
- Protein: 4g

LOW-CARB ZUCCHINI LOAF

Servings: 1 loaf

Preparation time: 20 minutes

Cook time: : 1 hour and 30 minutes

Ingredients

- Two ¼ cup almond flour
- 1 ½ cup zucchini, grated
- ¾ cup no-calorie sweetener of your choice
- ½ cup walnuts, chopped
- ½ cup pecans,

Directions

1. First, put the wet ingredients into the pan, followed by all dry ingredients.
2. Press the "Quick" or "Cake" mode of your bread machine.
3. Allow the machine to complete all the cycles.
4. Take out the pan from the machine, but keep the loaf in the pan for another 10 minutes.
5. Remove the loaf from the pan to let it cool down faster.
6. Slice and serve.

chopped

- Two tablespoons coconut flour
- Three teaspoons baking powder
- One teaspoon ground cinnamon
- ¼ teaspoon nutmeg
- ¼ teaspoon ginger, grated
- Five eggs, beaten
- ½ cup of coconut oil
- Two teaspoons vanilla extract

Nutrition Information

- Calories: 217
- Carbohydrates: 5g
- Fat: 15g
- Protein: 5g

CHUNKY CHOCOLATE LOAF

Servings: 1 loaf

Preparation time: 20 minutes

Cook time: : 1 hour and 30 minutes

Ingredients

- ½ cup coconut flour
- ¼ cup almond flour
- ¼ cup protein powder, unsweetened
- ½ cup no-calorie sweetener of your choice
- ¼ cup dark chocolate chunks, 70% cocoa solids
- ¼ cup dark cocoa

Directions

1. Put all wet ingredients first, then the dry ingredients into the bread pan.
2. Select the "Quick" or "Cake" setting of your bread machine.
3. Allow all cycles to be finished.
4. Remove the pan from the machine.
5. Wait for 10 minutes before taking out the loaf from the pan.
6. Let the loaf cool down completely before slicing it.

powder

- One teaspoon baking soda
- ½ teaspoon salt
- Six eggs
- ½ cup of coconut oil

Nutrition Information

- Calories: 206
- Carbohydrates: 6g
- Fat: 17g
- Protein: 6g

PEANUT BUTTER BREAD

Servings: 1 loaf

Preparation time: **15 minutes**

Cook time: : **3 hours**

Ingredients

- One ¾ cup almond flour
- 1 cup peanut butter, unsweetened and without oil
- 2/3 cup no-calorie sweetener of your choice
- 1/3 cup whole psyllium husk

Directions

1. Add the wet ingredients and followed by the dry ingredients to the bread pan.
2. Select the "Basic" or Normal" mode with a medium crust colour setting.
3. Allow the machine to finish the mixing kneading and baking cycles.
4. Take out the bread from the machine and the pan to cool it down.
5. Slice and serve.

- One tablespoon baking powder
- Two eggs
- ½ cup almond milk, unsweetened
- One teaspoon apple cider vinegar
- One teaspoon vanilla extract

Nutrition Information

- Calories: 186
- Carbohydrates: 8g
- Fat: 11g
- Protein: 6g

SWEET DINNER ROLLS

Servings: 1 loaf

Preparation time: **1 hour**

Cook time: : **30 minutes**

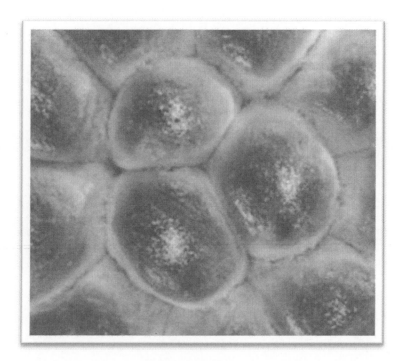

Ingredients

- 2 ½ cups almond flour
- 1 cup coconut flour
- ½ cup butter
- ¼ cup no-calorie sweetener of your

Directions

1. Add the wet ingredients into the bread pan, and then the dry ingredients.
2. Use the "Manual" or "Dough" mode of the bread machine.
3. Once done, put the dough in a lightly oiled bowl.
4. Preheat the oven to 3750F.
5. Divide and shape the dough into 16 pieces.

choice

- ¾ teaspoons salt
- Two eggs
- 1 cup milk

6. Cover and just let the dough rise for 30 minutes.
7. Bake until golden brown.
8. Cooldown and serve.

Nutrition Information

- Calories: 125
- Carbohydrates: 4g
- Fat: 9g
- Protein: 8g

KETO BREADSTICKS

Servings: 2 pcs

Preparation time: **3 hours**

Cook time: : **15-20 minutes**

Ingredients

- 1 ½ cup mozzarella cheese, shredded
- 1-ounce cream cheese
- ½ cup almond flour
- Three tablespoons coconut flour
- One egg
- ½ cup mozzarella cheese, shredded

Directions

1. Add the ingredients for the bread into the bread pan.
2. Put the bread machine on "Manual" or "Dough" mode.
3. After the cycles are finished, place the dough on a surface with a light dusting of flour.
4. Divide the dough into four and then divide each quarter again into 6.
5. Roll each piece until it is 8 inches long. Place the rolled dough on a greased baking sheet.
6. Brush over each piece with the egg wash.

- 1/3 cup parmesan cheese, shredded
- ¼ cup egg wash
- One teaspoon parsley, finely chopped

7. Cover, and allow it to rise for 10 minutes.
8. Preheat the oven t0 4000F.
9. Spread half of the toppings on each piece.
10. Bake for 5 minutes before spreading the remaining toppings on the breadsticks.
11. Bake for another 10 minutes, or until the cheese has melted.
12. Remove it and then let it cool down on a wire rack.

Nutrition Information

- Calories: 207
- Carbohydrates: 7g
- Fat: 14g
- Protein: 13g

KETO FOCACCIA BREAD

Servings: 1 loaf

Preparation time: **3 hours**

Cook time: : **23-30 minutes**

Ingredients

- 1 cup almond flour
- 1/3 cup coconut flour
- 1/3 cup protein powder, unflavored and unsweetened

Directions

1. Place the wet ingredients first in the bread pan, followed by the dry ingredients.
2. Set the bread machine to "Manual" or "Dough" mode.
3. Once the cycles are completed, put the dough on a surface with a light dusting of flour.

- Two tablespoons rosemary, chopped
- One tablespoon baking powder
- ¾ teaspoon salt
- ½ teaspoon garlic powder
- Two eggs, whole
- Two egg whites
- ½ cup extra-virgin olive oil
- ½ cup of water

4. Shape the dough into a ball.
5. Flatten the dough on a greased baking sheet until it becomes a 10-inch circle.
6. Cover the dough, and allow it to rise for 15 minutes.
7. Preheat the oven to 3750F.
8. Bake for 25 to 30 minutes.

Nutrition Information

- Calories: 174 Cal
- Carbohydrates: 5 g
- Fat: 15g

Chapter 10: Regular Bread

CLASSIC WHITE BREAD

Servings: 1 loaf

Preparation time: **2 hours**

Cook time: : **1 hour and 30 minutes**

Ingredients

- ½ cup (110 ml) lukewarm whole milk
- 1 cup (210 ml) lukewarm water
- 2 tbsp. white sugar
- 1 tbsp. butter, melted

Directions

1. Place all the dry and liquid ingredients in the pan and follow the instructions for your bread machine.

2. Pay particular attention to measuring the ingredients. Use a cup, measuring spoon, and kitchen scales to do so.

3. Set the baking program to BASIC also set the crust type to MEDIUM.

4. If the dough is too wet, adjust the bread machine and cool

- 1 tsp. salt
- 3½ cups (450 g) wheat bread machine/white/all-purpose flour
- 2 tbsp. bread machine yeast

for five minutes.

5. Shake the loaf out of the pan. If necessary, use a spatula.

6. Wrap the bread with a kitchen towel and set it aside for an hour. Otherwise, you'll calm on a wire rack.

Nutrition Information

- Calories 240
- Total Fat 2.4g
- Cholesterol 5g
- Carbohydrate 46.6g
- Dietary Fiber 2.1g
- Total Sugars 3.8g
- Protein 7.3g

COCONUT BRAN BREAD

Servings: 1 loaf

Preparation time: 2 hours

Cook time: : 1 hour and 30 minutes

Ingredients

- 3¾ cups (480 g) wheat bread machine / white flour
- 1¾ cups (200 g) bran meal
- 1¼ cups (300 ml) cream
- 1/3 cup (70 ml) coconut milk

Directions

1. Place all the dry and liquid ingredients in the pan and follow the instructions for your bread

2. Pay particular attention to measuring the ingredients. Use a cup, measuring spoon, and kitchen scales to do so.

3. Set the baking program to BASIC also set the crust type to MEDIUM.

4. If the dough is too wet, adjust the bread machine and cool for five minutes.

5. Wrap the bread with a kitchen towel and set it aside for

- 2 Tbsp. liquid honey

- 2 Tbsp. vegetable oil

- 2 tsp. salt

an hour. Otherwise, you'll calm on a wire rack.

Nutrition Information

- Calories 348
- Total Fat 8.6g
- Saturated Fat 4.2g
- Cholesterol 7g
- Carbohydrate 59.4g
- Dietary Fiber 3.2g
- Total Sugars 6.7g
- Protein 8.1g

MILK WHITE BREAD

Servings: 1 loaf

Preparation time: 2 hours

Cook time: : 3 hours and 30 minutes

Ingredients

- 1¼ cups (280 ml / 9½ oz.) Lukewarm whole milk
- 5¼ cups (680 g) wheat bread machine flour
- 2 tbsp. vegetable oil
- 2 tbsp. sour cream
- 2 tsp. bread machine yeast
- 1 tbsp. white sugar
- 2 tsp. salt

Directions

1. Place all the dry and liquid ingredients in the pan and follow the instructions for your bread machine.
2. Pay particular attention to measuring the ingredients. Use a cup, measuring spoon, and
3. kitchen scales to do so.
4. Set the baking program to BASIC also set the crust type to MEDIUM.
5. If the dough is too wet, adjust the
6. After mixing the dough thoroughly, smear the surface of the merchandise with soured cream.
7. When the program has ended, take the pan out of the bread machine and cool for five minutes.

8. Shake the loaf out of the pan. If necessary, use a spatula.

9. Wrap the bread with a kitchen towel and set it aside for an hour or, you can make it cool on a wire rack.

10. Cool, serve, and luxuriate.

Nutrition Information

- Calories 344
- Total Fat 4.9g
- Saturated Fat 1.2g
- Cholesterol 1g
- Carbohydrate 64.6g
- Total Sugars 1.7g
- Protein 8.9g

VANILLA MILK BREAD

Servings: 1 loaf

Preparation time: **2 hours**

Cook time: : **3 hours and 30 minutes**

Ingredients

- 4½ cups (580 g) wheat bread machine flour
- 1¾ cups (370 ml / 12½ oz.) lukewarm whole milk
- 1 tbsp. white sugar
- One packet vanilla sugar
- 2 tbsp. extra-virgin

Directions

1. Place all the dry and liquid ingredients in the pan and follow the instructions for your bread machine.
2. Pay particular attention to measuring the ingredients. Use a cup, measuring spoon, and kitchen scales to do so.
3. 3.Set, the baking program to BASIC, also set the crust type to MEDIUM.
4. If the dough is too wet, adjust the recipe's flour and liquid quantity.
5. When the program has ended, take the pan out of the bread machine and cool for five minutes.

olive oil

- 2 tsp. bread machine yeast

- 2 tsp. sea salt

6. Shake the loaf out of the pan. If necessary, use a spatula.

7. Wrap the bread with a kitchen towel and set it aside for an hour. Otherwise, you'll calm on a wire rack.

Nutrition Information

- Calories 328
- Total Fat 5.7g
- Saturated Fat 1.4g
- Cholesterol 4g
- Sodium 610mg
- Carbohydrate 59.1g
- Dietary Fiber 2.1g
- Total Sugars 4.6g
- Protein 9.4g

CORN BREAD

Servings: 1 loaf

Preparation time: **2 hours**

Cook time: : **3 hours and 30 minutes**

Ingredients

- 3½ cups (480 g) cornflour
- 1½ cups (200 g) bread machine wheat flour,
- sifted
- 2 tbsp. butter softened

Directions

1. Place all the dry and liquid ingredients in the pan and follow the instructions for your bread machine.

2. Pay particular attention to measuring the ingredients. Use a cup, measuring spoon, and kitchen scales to do so.

3. Set the baking program to primary also set the crust type to medium.

4. If the dough is too wet, adjust the recipe's flour and liquid quantity.

5. After mixing the dough thoroughly, moisten the

- ½ cup cornflakes
- 1 tbsp. white sugar
- 2 tsp. Bread machine yeast
- 2 tsp. salt

merchandise's surface with water and sprinkle with cornflakes.

6. When the program has ended, take the pan out of the bread machine and cool for five minutes.

7. Shake the loaf out of the pan. If necessary, use a spatula.

8. Wrap the bread with a kitchen towel and set it aside for an hour. Otherwise, you'll calm on a wire rack.

Nutrition Information

- Calories 319
- total fat 5.1g
- saturated fat 2.1g
- cholesterol 8g
- sodium 634mg
- Carbohydrate 62.3g
- dietary fibre 4.8g
- total sugars 2.1g
- protein 7.3g

CREAM HAZELNUT BREAD

Servings: 1 loaf

Preparation time: **1 hour and 30 minutes**

Cook time: : **1 hour**

Ingredients

- 3½ cups (450 g) wheat bread machine flour
- 1¾ cups (230 g) cornflour
- 5 ounces (150 ml) cream
- 2 tbsp. vegetable oil
- 2 tsp. bread machine yeast

Directions

1. Place all the dry and liquid ingredients in the pan and follow the instructions for your bread machine.
2. Pay particular attention to measuring the ingredients. Use a cup, measuring spoon, and
3. kitchen scales to do so.
4. Set the baking program to BASIC also set the crust type to MEDIUM.
5. If the dough is too wet, adjust the recipe's flour and liquid quantity.
6. After the dough finishes mixing moisten the merchandise's surface with water and

- 1 tbsp. sugar
- ½ cup hazelnuts, ground
- 2 tsp. sea salt

sprinkle with hazelnut.

7. When the program has ended, take the pan out of the bread machine and cool for five minutes.

8. Shake the loaf out of the pan. If necessary, use a spatula.

9. Wrap the bread with a kitchen towel and set it aside for an hour. Otherwise, you'll calm on a wire rack.

Nutrition Information

- Calories: 405 Cal
- Fat: 11.8 g
- Cholesterol: 13 g
- Sodium: 607 mg
- Carbohydrates: 66.3 g
- Fiber: 4 g

Chapter 11: Bread Perfect for Dinner

CORN POPPY SEEDS SOUR CREAM BREAD

Servings: 1 loaf (16 slices)

Preparation time: **2 hours**

Cook time: : **1 hour and 30 minutes**

Ingredients

- 3½ cups all-purpose flour
- 1¾ cups of cornflour
- 5 ounces sour cream
- Two tablespoons corn

Directions

1. Select the program of your bread machine to BASIC and choose the crust colour to MEDIUM.
2. Press START.
3. After the kneading brush the loaf with the water and sprinkle with poppy

oil

- Two teaspoons active dry yeast
- Two teaspoons salt
- 16 ¼ ounces lukewarm water
- poppy seeds for sprinkling

seeds.

4. Wait until the program completes.
5. When done, take the bucket out and let it cool for 5-10 minutes.
6. Shake the loaf from the pan and let cool for 30 minutes on a cooling rack.
7. Slice, serve and enjoy the taste of fragrant homemade bread.

Nutrition Information

- Calories 223
- Total Fat 4.8g
- Saturated Fat 1.6g
- Cholesterol 4g
- Sodium 297mg
- Total Carbohydrate 39.9g
- Total Sugars 0.2g
- Protein 5.2g

OATMEAL BREAD

Servings: 1 loaf (12 slices)

Preparation time: 2 hours

Cook time: : 3 hours

Ingredients

- 1 ½ teaspoon active dry yeast
- 2 cups (350 g) white bread flour, sifted
- ½ cup (100 g) oatmeal flour
- One teaspoon salt
- Two tablespoons liquid honey (can be

Directions

1. Prepare all of the ingredients for your bread and measuring means (a cup, a spoon, kitchen scales).
2. Carefully measure the ingredients into the pan.
3. Place all of the ingredients into a bread bucket in the right order and follow your bread machine's manual.
4. Close the cover.
5. Select the program of your bread machine to BASIC and choose the crust colour to MEDIUM.
6. Press START.

replaced with sugar)

- ½ cup (150 ml) yogurt
- One tablespoon butter, melted
- ¾ cup (200 ml) lukewarm water (80 degrees F)
- Two tablespoons oatmeal flakes

7. After the kneading lubricate the loaf's surface water or egg yolk and sprinkle with oat flakes.

8. Wait until the program completes.

9. When done, take the bucket out and let it cool for 5-10 minutes.

10. Shake the loaf from the pan and let cool for 30 minutes on a cooling rack.

11. Slice, serve and enjoy the taste of fragrant homemade bread.

Nutrition Information

- Calories 176
- Total Fat 2.3g
- Saturated Fat 1.2g
- Sodium 313mg
- Total Carbohydrate 32.9g
- Dietary Fiber 1.6g
- Total Sugars 5.5g
- Protein 5.5g

SIMPLE DARK RYE BREAD

Servings: 1 loaf (8 slices)

Preparation time: 1 hour

Cook time: : 2 hours

Ingredients

- 2/3 cup lukewarm water (80 degrees F)
- One tablespoon melted butter cooled
- ¼ cup molasses
- ¼ teaspoon salt
- One tablespoon unsweetened cocoa

Directions

1. Prepare all of the ingredients for your bread and measuring means (a cup, a spoon, kitchen scales).
2. Carefully measure the ingredients into the pan.
3. Place all of the ingredients into the bread bucket in the right order and follow your bread machine's manual.
4. Close the cover.
5. Select the program of your bread machine to BASIC and choose the crust colour to MEDIUM.

- powder
- ½ cup rye flour
- pinch of ground nutmeg
- 1¼ cups white wheat flour sifted
- 1 1/8 teaspoons active dry yeast

6. Wait until the program completes.
7. When done, take the bucket out and let it cool for 5-10 minutes.
8. Shake the loaf from the pan and let cool for 30 minutes on a cooling rack.
9. Slice, serve and enjoy the taste of fragrant homemade bread.

Nutrition Information

- Calories 151
- Total Fat 2.1g
- Saturated Fat 1g
- Cholesterol 4g
- Sodium 88mg
- Total Carbohydrate 29.4g
- Dietary Fiber 2.7g
- Total Sugars 5.9g
- Protein 4.2g

WALNUT BREAD

Servings: 1 loaf (20 slices)

Preparation time: **2 hours**

Cook time: : **2 hours**

Ingredients

- 4 cups (500 g) wheat flour, sifted
- ½ cup (130 ml) lukewarm water (80 degrees F)
- ½ cup (120 ml) lukewarm milk (80 degrees F)
- Two whole eggs
- ½ cup walnuts, fried

Directions

1. Prepare all of the ingredients for your bread and measuring means (a cup, a spoon, kitchen scales).
2. Carefully measure the ingredients into the pan.
3. Place all of the ingredients into the bread bucket in the right order. Follow your manual bread machine.
4. Close the cover.
5. Select your bread machine's program to FRENCH BREAD and choose the crust colour to MEDIUM.
6. Press START.

and chopped

- One tablespoon walnut oil
- One tablespoon brown sugar
- One teaspoon salt
- One teaspoon active dry yeast

7. Wait until the program completes.

8. When done, take the bucket out and let it cool for 5-10 minutes.

9. Shake the loaf from the pan and let cool for 30 minutes on a cooling rack.

10. Slice, serve and enjoy the taste of fragrant homemade bread.

Nutrition Information

- Calories 257
- Total Fat 6.7g
- Saturated Fat 1g
- Cholesterol 34g
- Sodium 252mg
- Total Carbohydrate 40.8g
- Total Sugars 2g
- Protein 8.3g

MULTIGRAIN BREAD

Servings: 1 loaf (8 slices)

Preparation time: **1 hour**

Cook time: : **2 hours**

Ingredients

- One tablespoon melted butter
- ½ tablespoon liquid honey
- ½ teaspoon salt
- ¾ cup multigrain flour
- 1 1/3 cups wheat flour
- One teaspoon active

Directions

1. Prepare all of the ingredients for your bread and measuring means (a cup, a spoon, kitchen scales).
2. Carefully measure the ingredients into the pan.
3. Place all of your ingredients into the bread bucket in the right order. Follow your manual bread machine.
4. Close the cover.
5. Select your bread machine's program to FRENCH BREAD and choose the crust colour to MEDIUM.
6. Press START.

dry yeast

7. Wait until the program completes.

8. When done, take the bucket out and let it cool for 5-10 minutes.

9. Shake the loaf from the pan and let cool for 30 minutes on a cooling rack.

10. Slice, serve and enjoy the taste of fragrant homemade bread.

Nutrition Information

- Calories 124
- Total Fat 2.8g
- Saturated Fat 1.1g
- Cholesterol 4g
- Sodium 207mg
- Total Carbohydrate 22.8g
- Total Sugars 1.5g
- Protein 4.6g

SAUERKRAUT BREAD

Servings: 1 loaf (22 slices)

Preparation time: **2 hour**

Cook time: : **1 hour and 30 minutes**

Ingredients

- 1 cup lukewarm water (80 degrees F)
- ¼ cup cabbage brine
- ½ cup finely chopped cabbage
- Two tablespoons sunflower oil
- Two teaspoons white

Directions

1. Prepare all of the ingredients for your bread and measuring means (a cup, a spoon, kitchen scales).
2. Finely chop the sauerkraut.
3. Carefully measure the ingredients into the pan.
4. Place all of the ingredients into a bucket in the right order, follow your manual bread machine.
5. Close the cover.
6. Select the program of your bread machine to BASIC and

sugar

- 1½ teaspoons salt
- 2 1/3 cups rye flour
- 2 1/3 cups wheat flour
- Two teaspoons dry kvass
- Two teaspoons active dry yeast

choose the crust colour to DARK.

7. Press START.
8. Wait until the program completes.
9. When done, take the bucket out and let it cool for 5-10 minutes.
10. Shake the loaf from the pan and let cool for 30 minutes on a cooling rack.
11. Slice, serve and enjoy the taste of fragrant homemade bread.

Nutrition Information

- Calories 297
- Total Fat 4.9g
- Saturated Fat 0.5g
- Cholesterol 0g
- Sodium 442mg
- Total Carbohydrate 55.5g
- Dietary Fiber 9.7g
- Total Sugars 1.6g
- Protein 9.5g

RICE BREAD

Ingredients

- 4½ cups all-purpose flour
- 1 cup of rice, cooked
- One whole egg beaten
- Two tablespoons of milk powder
- Two teaspoons active

Directions

1. Prepare all of the ingredients for your bread and measuring means (a cup, a spoon, kitchen scales).
2. Carefully measure the ingredients into the pan.
3. Place all of the ingredients into a bread bucket in the right order, follow your manual bread machine.
4. Close the cover.
5. Select the program of your bread machine to BASIC and choose the crust colour to MEDIUM.

- dry yeast
- Two tablespoons butter, melted
- One tablespoon sugar
- Two teaspoon salt
- 1¼ cups lukewarm water (80 degrees F)

6. Press START.
7. Wait until the program completes.
8. When done, take the bucket out and let it cool for 5-10 minutes.
9. Shake the loaf from the pan and let cool for 30 minutes on a cooling rack.
10. Slice, serve and enjoy the taste of fragrant homemade bread.

Nutrition Information

- Calories 197
- Total Fat 2.1g
- Saturated Fat 1.1g
- Cholesterol 14g
- Sodium 311mg
- Total Carbohydrate 37.8g
- Dietary Fiber 1.3g
- Total Sugars 1.4g
- Protein 5.6g

RICE WHEAT BREAD

Servings: 1 loaf (22 slices)

Preparation time: **2 hour**

Cook time: : **1 hour and 30 minutes**

Ingredients

- 4½ cups (580 g) wheat bread flour
- 1 cup (200 g) rice, cooked
- One whole egg
- Two tablespoons soy sauce
- Two teaspoons active dried yeast

Directions

1. Prepare all of the ingredients for your bread and measuring means (a cup, a spoon, kitchen scales).
2. Carefully measure the ingredients into the pan.
3. Place all of the ingredients into a bucket in the right order. Follow your manual for the bread machine.
4. Close the cover.
5. Select the program of your bread machine to BASIC and choose the crust colour to MEDIUM.
6. Press START.

- Two tablespoons melted butter
- One tablespoon brown sugar
- Two teaspoons kosher salt

7. Wait until the program completes.
8. When done, take the bucket out and let it cool for 5-10 minutes.
9. Shake the loaf from the pan and let cool for 30 minutes on a cooling rack.
10. Slice, serve and enjoy the taste of fragrant homemade bread.

Nutrition Information

- Calories 321
- Total Fat 4.2g
- Saturated Fat 2.1g
- Cholesterol 28g
- Sodium 837mg
- Total Carbohydrate 60.4g
- Dietary Fiber 2.2g
- Total Sugars 1.4g
- Protein 9.1g

PEPPER BREAD

Servings: 1 loaf (8 slices)

Preparation time: **2 hour**

Cook time: : **1 hour and 10 minutes**

Ingredients

- ¾ cup + 1 tablespoon lukewarm milk
- Three tablespoons ground red pepper
- Four teaspoons fresh red pepper, chopped and roasted
- Two tablespoons

Directions

1. Prepare all of the ingredients for your bread and measuring means (a cup, a spoon, kitchen scales).

2. Carefully measure the ingredients into the pan.

3. Place all of the ingredients into a bucket in the right order. Follow your manual for the bread machine.

4. Close the cover.

5. Select the program of your bread machine to BASIC and choose the crust colour to MEDIUM.

- butter, melted
- Two tablespoons brown sugar
- 2/3 teaspoon salt
- 2 cups wheat flour
- One teaspoon active dry yeast

6. Press START.
7. Wait until the program completes.
8. When done, take the bucket out and let it cool for 5-10 minutes.
9. Shake the loaf from the pan and let cool for 30 minutes on a cooling rack.
10. Slice, serve and enjoy the taste of fragrant homemade bread.

Nutrition Information

- Calories: 189
- Fat: 4.5 g
- Cholesterol: 10 g
- Sodium: 34 mg
- Carbohydrates: 33 g
- Fiber: 2.3 g
- Sugar: 6.8 g
- Protein: 5.1 g

Chapter 12: Vegan Bread

BANANA LEMON LOAF

Servings: 1 loaf (16 slices)

Preparation time: **15 minutes**

Cook time: : **1 hour and 30 minutes**

Ingredients

- 2 cups all-purpose flour
- 1 cup bananas, very ripe and mashed
- 1 cup walnuts, chopped
- 1 cup of sugar

Directions

1. Put all ingredients into a pan in this order: bananas, wet ingredients, and then dry ingredients.
2. Press the "Quick" or "Cake" setting of your bread machine.
3. Allow the cycles to be completed.
4. Take out the pan from the machine. The cooldown for 10 minutes before slicing the bread enjoy.

- One tablespoon baking powder
- One teaspoon lemon peel, grated
- ½ teaspoon salt
- Two eggs
- ½ cup of vegetable oil
- Two tablespoons lemon juice

Nutrition Information

- Calories: 120
- Carbohydrates: 15g
- Fat: 6g
- Protein: 2g

MULTIGRAIN OLIVE OIL WHITE BREAD

Servings: 1 loaf (16 slices)

Preparation time: **15 minutes**

Cook time: : **1 hour and 30 minutes**

Ingredients

- For the Dough
- 300 ml water
- 500 grams bakers flour
- 8 grams dried yeast
- 10 ml salt
- 5 ml caster suger
- 40 ml olive oil
- For the Seed mix

Directions

1. For the water: to 100ml of boiling water add 200ml of cold water.
2. Add the ingredients in the order required by the manufacturer.
3. add the seeds at the time required by your machine.
4. Empty dough onto a floured surface and gently use your finger tips to push some of the air out of it. Shape however you like and place on or in an oiled baking tray. Sprinkle with flour or brush with egg for a glazed finish. Slash the top. Cover and rise for 30 mins.

- 40 grams sunflower seeds
- 20 grams sesame seeds
- 20 grams flax seeds
- 20 grams quinoa
- 20 grams pumpkin seeds

5. Heat oven to 240C/220C fan/gas 8. Bake for 30-35 mins until browned and crisp.

Nutrition Information

- Calories 114.1
- Total Fat 3.1 g
- Saturated Fat 0.5 g
- Polyunsaturated Fat 0.4 g
- Monounsaturated Fat 1.9 g
- Sodium 83.4 mg
- Potassium 0.0 mg
- Total Carbohydrate 19.7 g

ORANGE DATE BREAD

Servings: 1 loaf

Preparation time: **20 minutes**

Cook time: : **1 hour and 30 minutes**

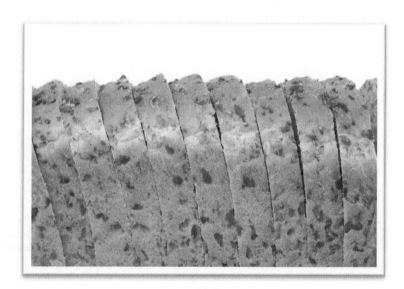

Ingredients

- 2 cups all-purpose flour
- 1 cup dates, chopped
- ¾ cup of sugar
- ½ cup walnuts, chopped
- Two tablespoons orange rind, grated
- 1 ½ teaspoons baking powder

Directions

1. Put the wet ingredients then the dry ingredients into the bread pan.
2. Press the "Quick" or "Cake" mode of the bread machine.
3. Allow all cycles to be finished.
4. Remove the pan from the machine, but keep the bread in the pan for 10 minutes more.
5. Take out the bread from the pan, and let it cool down completely before slicing.

- One teaspoon baking soda
- ½ cup of orange juice
- ½ cup of water
- One tablespoon vegetable oil
- One teaspoon vanilla extract

Nutrition Information

- Calories: 80
- Carbohydrates: 14g
- Fat: 2g
- Protein: 1g

ZERO-FAT CARROT AND PINAPPLE LOAF

Servings: 1 loaf

Preparation time: **20 minutes**

Cook time: : **1 hour and 30 minutes**

Ingredients

- 2 ½ cups all-purpose flour
- ¾ cup of sugar
- ½ cup pineapples, crushed
- ½ cup carrots, grated
- ½ cup raisins
- Two teaspoons baking powder
- ½ teaspoon ground

Directions

1. Put first the wet ingredients into the bread pan before the dry ingredients.
2. Press the "Quick" or "Cake" mode of your bread machine.
3. Allow the machine to complete all cycles.
4. Take out the pan from the machine, but wait for another 10 minutes before transferring the bread into a wire rack.
5. Cooldown the bread before slicing.

cinnamon

- ½ teaspoon salt
- ¼ teaspoon allspice
- ¼ teaspoon nutmeg
- ½ cup applesauce
- One tablespoon molasses

Nutrition Information

- Calories: 70
- Carbohydrates: 16g
- Fat: 0g
- Protein: 1g

AUTUMN TREASURES LOAF

Servings: 1 loaf

Preparation time: **15 minutes**

Cook time: : **1 hour and 30 minutes**

Ingredients

- 1 cup all-purpose flour
- ½ cup dried fruit, chopped
- ¼ cup pecans, chopped
- ¼ cup of sugar
- Two tablespoons baking powder
- One teaspoon salt

Directions

1. Add all wet ingredients first to the bread pan before the dry ingredients.
2. Turn on the bread machine with the "Quick" or "Cake" setting.
3. Wait for all cycles to be finished.
4. Remove the bread pan from the machine.
5. After 10 minutes, transfer the bread from the pan into a wire rack.
6. Slice the bread only when it has completely cooled down.

- ¼ teaspoon of baking soda
- ½ teaspoon ground nutmeg
- 1 cup apple juice
- ¼ cup of vegetable oil
- Three tablespoons aquafaba
- One teaspoon of vanilla extract

Nutrition Information

- Calories: 80
- Carbohydrates: 12g
- Fat: 3g
- Protein: 1g

OATMEAL WALNUT BREAD

Servings: 1 loaf

Preparation time: **15 minutes**

Cook time: : **1 hour and 30 minutes**

Ingredients

- ¾ cup whole-wheat flour
- ¼ cup all-purpose flour

Directions

1. Add into the bread pan the wet ingredients then followed by the dry ingredients.
2. Use the "Quick" or "Cake" setting of your bread machine.
3. Allow the cycles to be completed.

- ½ cup brown sugar
- 1/3 cup walnuts, chopped
- ¼ cup oatmeal
- ¼ teaspoon of baking soda
- Two tablespoons baking powder
- One teaspoon salt
- 1 cup Vegan buttermilk
- ¼ cup of vegetable oil
- Three tablespoons aquafaba

4. Take out the pan from the machine.
5. Wait for 10 minutes, then remove the bread from the pan.
6. Once the bread has cooled down, slice it and serve.

Nutrition Information

- Calories: 80
- Carbohydrates: 11g
- Fat: 3g
- Protein: 2g

PUMPKIN RAISIN BREAD

Servings: 1 loaf

Preparation time: **15 minutes**

Cook time: : **1 hour and 30 minutes**

Ingredients

- ½ cup all-purpose flour
- ½ cup whole-wheat flour
- ½ cup pumpkin, mashed
- ½ cup raisins
- ¼ cup brown sugar

Directions

1. Place all ingredients in the bread pan in this order: apple juice, pumpkin, oil, aquafaba, flour, sugar, baking powder, baking soda, salt, pumpkin pie spice, and raisins.
2. Select the "Quick" or "Cake" mode of your bread machine.
3. Let the machine finish all cycles.
4. Remove the pan from the machine.
5. After 10 minutes, transfer the bread to a wire rack.

- Two tablespoons baking powder
- One teaspoon salt
- One teaspoon pumpkin pie spice
- ¼ teaspoon baking soda
- ¾ cup apple juice
- ¼ cup of vegetable oil
- Three tablespoons aquafaba

6. Slice the bread only when it has completely cooled down.

Nutrition Information

- Calories: 70
- Carbohydrates: 12g
- Fat: 2g
- Protein: 1g

HAWAIIAN BREAD

Servings: 1 loaf

Preparation time: 10 minutes

Cook time: : 3 hours

Ingredients

- 3 cups bread flour
- 2 ½ tablespoons brown sugar
- ¾ teaspoon salt
- Two teaspoons quick-rising yeast
- One egg
- ¾ cup pineapple juice
- Two tablespoons almond milk

Directions

1. Pour all wet ingredients first into the bread pan before adding the dry ingredients.
2. Set the bread machine to "Basic" or "Normal" mode with a light crust colour setting.
3. Allow the machine to finish the mixing kneading and baking cycles.
4. Take out the pan from the machine.
5. Transfer the bread to a wire rack.
6. After one hour, slice the bread and serve.

- Two tablespoons
  vegetable oil

Nutrition Information

- Calories: 169
- Carbohydrates: 30g
- Fat: 3g
- Protein: 4g

SWEET POTATO BREAD

Servings: 1 loaf

Preparation time: **10 minutes**

Cook time: : **3 hours**

Ingredients

- 4 cups bread flour
- 1 cup sweet potatoes, mashed
- ½ cup brown sugar
- Two teaspoons yeast
- 1 ½ teaspoon salt
- ½ teaspoon cinnamon

Directions

1. Add the wet ingredients first, then follow by dry ingredients to the bread pan.
2. Use the "Normal" or "Basic" mode of the bread machine.
3. Select the light or medium crust colour setting.
4. Once the cycles are finished, take out the machine's bread, Cooldown the bread on a wire rack before slicing and serving.

- ½ cup of water
- Two tablespoons vegetable oil
- One teaspoon vanilla extract

Nutrition Information

- Calories: 111
- Carbohydrates: 21g
- Fat: 2g
- Protein: 3g

BLACK FOREST LOAF

Servings: 1 loaf

Preparation time: **20 minutes**

Cook time: : **3 hours**

Ingredients

- 1 ½ cups bread flour
- 1 cup whole wheat flour
- 1 cup rye flour
- Three tablespoons cocoa
- One tablespoon caraway seeds
- Two teaspoons yeast

Directions

1. Combine the ingredients in the bread pan by putting the wet ingredients first, followed by the dry ones.
2. Press the "Normal" or "Basic" mode and light the bread machine's crust colour setting.
3. After the cycles are completed, take out the bread from the machine.
4. Cooldown and then slice the bread.

- 1 ½ teaspoons salt
- One ¼ cups water
- 1/3 cup molasses
- 1 ½ tablespoon canola oil

Nutrition Information

- Calories: 136
- Carbohydrates: 27g
- Fat: 2g
- Protein: 3g

VEGAN CINNAMON RAISIN BREAD

Servings: 1 loaf

Preparation time: 20 minutes

Cook time: : 3 hours

Ingredients

- Two ¼ cups oat flour
- ¾ cup raisins
- ½ cup almond flour
- ¼ cup of coconut sugar
- 2 ½ teaspoons cinnamon
- One teaspoon baking powder
- ½ teaspoon baking

Directions

1. Put all wet ingredients first into the bread pan, followed by the dry ingredients.
2. Set the bread machine to "Quick" or "Cake" mode.
3. Wait until the mixing and baking cycles are done.
4. Remove the pan from the machine.
5. Wait for another 10 minutes before transferring the bread to a wire rack.
6. After the bread has completely cooled down, slice it and serve.

soda

- ¼ teaspoon salt
- ¾ cup of water
- ½ cup of soy milk
- ¼ cup maple syrup
- Three tablespoons coconut oil
- One teaspoon vanilla extract

Nutrition Information

- Calories: 130
- Carbohydrates: 26g
- Fat: 2g
- Protein: 3g

BEER BREAD

Servings: 1 loaf

Preparation time: **10-15 minutes**

Cook time: : **2.5-3 hours**

Ingredients

- 3 cups bread flour
- Two tablespoons sugar
- Two ¼ teaspoons yeast
- 1 ½ teaspoons salt
- 2/3 cup beer
- 1/3 cup water
- Two tablespoons vegetable oil

Directions

1. Add all ingredients into a pan in this order: water, beer, oil, salt, sugar, flour, and yeast.
2. Start the bread machine with the "Basic" or "Normal" mode on and light to medium crust colour.
3. Let the machine complete all cycles.
4. Take out the pan from the machine.
5. Transfer the beer bread into a wire rack to cool it down for about an hour.
6. Cut into 12 slices, and serve.

Nutrition Information

- Calories: 130
- Carbohydrates: 25g
- Fat: 1g
- Protein: 4g

ONION AND MUSHROOM BREAD

Servings: 1 loaf

Preparation time: **10 minutes**

Cook time: : **1 hour**

Ingredients

- 4 ounces mushrooms, chopped
- 4 cups bread flour
- Three tablespoons sugar
- Four teaspoons fast-acting yeast
- Four teaspoons dried onions, minced
- 1 ½ teaspoons salt

Directions

1. Pour the water first into the bread pan, and then add all of the dry ingredients.
2. Press the "Fast" cycle mode of the bread machine.
3. Wait until all cycles are completed.
4. Transfer the bread from the pan into a wire rack.
5. Wait for one hour before slicing the bread into 12 pieces.
6. Servings: 2 ounces per slice

- ½ teaspoon garlic powder
- ¾ cup of water

Nutrition Information

- Calories: 120
- Carbohydrates: 25g
- Fat: 0g
- Protein: 5g

LOW-CARB MULTIGRAIN BREAD

Servings: 1 loaf

Preparation time: 15 minutes

Cook time: : 1 hour and 30 minutes

Ingredients

- ¾ cup whole-wheat flour
- ¼ cup cornmeal
- ¼ cup oatmeal
- Two tablespoons 7-grain cereals
- Two tablespoons baking powder
- One teaspoon salt
- ¼ teaspoon baking

Directions

1. In the bread pan, add the wet ingredients first, then the dry ingredients.
2. Press the "Quick" or "Cake" mode of your bread machine.
3. Wait until all cycles are through.
4. Remove the bread pan from the machine.
5. Let the bread rest for 10 minutes in the pan before taking it out to cool down further.
6. Slice the bread after an hour has passed.

soda

- ¾ cup of water
- ¼ cup of vegetable oil
- ¼ cup of orange juice
- Three tablespoons aquafaba

Nutrition Information

- Calories: 60
- Carbohydrates: 9g
- Fat: 2g
- Protein: 1g

MASHED POTATO BREAD

Servings: 1 loaf

Preparation time: **40 minutes**

Cook time: : **2.5-3 hours**

Ingredients

- 2 1/3 cups bread flour
- ½ cup mashed potatoes
- One tablespoon sugar
- 1 ½ teaspoons yeast
- ¾ teaspoon salt
- ¼ cup potato water
- One tablespoon

Directions

1. Put the ingredients into the pan in this order: potato water, oil, flax seeds, mashed potatoes, sugar, salt, flour, and yeast.
2. Ready the bread machine by pressing the "Basic" or "Normal" mode with a medium crust colour setting.
3. Allow the bread machine to finish all cycles.
4. Remove the bread pan from the machine.
5. Carefully take the bread from the pan.
6. Put the bread on a wire rack, then cool down before slicing.

ground flax seeds

- Four teaspoons oil

Nutrition Information

- Calories: 140
- Carbohydrates: 26 g

Chapter 13: Basic Bread

BASIC WHITE BREAD

Servings: 1 loaf

Preparation time: 1 hour and 15 minutes

Cook time: : 50 minutes (20+30 minutes)

Ingredients

- ½ to 5/8 cup Water
- 5/8 cup Milk
- 1 ½ tablespoon butter or margarine
- Three tablespoon Sugar

Directions

1. Put all ingredients in the bread pan, using a minimal measure of liquid listed in the recipe. Select medium Crust setting and press Start.

2. Observe the dough as it kneads. Following 5 to 10 minutes, if it seems dry and firm, or if your machine seems as though it's straining to knead, add more liquid one tablespoon at a time until dough forms well.

- 1 ½ teaspoon Salt
- 3 cups Bread Flour
- 1 ½ teaspoon Active dry yeast

3. Once the baking cycle ends, remove bread from the pan and cool before slicing.

Nutrition Information

- Calories: 64 Cal
- Fat: 1 g
- Carbohydrates:12 g
- Protein: 2 g

GLUTEN-FREE BREAD

Servings: 1 loaf

Preparation time: **4 hours and 50 minutes**

Cook time: : **50 minutes (20+30 minutes)**

Ingredients

- 2 cups rice flour, Potato starch
- 1 1/2 cup Tapioca flour
- 1/2 cup Xanthan gum
- 2 1/2 teaspoons 2/3 cup powdered milk or 1/2 non-dairy substitute

Directions

1. Add yeast to the bread pan.
2. Add all the flours, xanthan/ gum, milk powder, salt, and sugar.
3. Beat the eggs, and mix with water, butter, and vinegar.
4. Choose white bread setting at medium or use a 3-4 hour set.

- 1 1/2 teaspoons salt
- 1 1/2 teaspoons egg substitute (optional)
- Three tablespoons Sugar
- 1 2/3 cups lukewarm water
- 1 1/2 tablespoons dry yeast, granules
- Four tablespoons butter, melted or margarine
- One teaspoon Vinegar
- Three eggs, room temperature

Nutrition Information

- Calories: 126 Cal
- Fat: 2 g
- Carbohydrates:29 g
- Protein: 3 g

ALL-PURPOSE WHITE BREAD

Servings: 1 loaf

Preparation time: 2 hours and 10 minutes

Cook time: : 40 minutes

Ingredients

- ¾ cup water at 80 degrees F
- One tablespoon melted butter cooled
- One tablespoon sugar
- ¾ teaspoon salt
- Two tablespoons skim milk powder
- 2 cups white bread flour
- ¾ teaspoon instant yeast

Directions

1. Add all of the ingredients to your bread machine, carefully following the instructions of the manufacturer.
2. Set the program of your bread machine to Basic/White Bread and set crust type to Medium.
3. Press START.
4. Wait until the cycle completes.
5. Once the loaf is ready, take the bucket out and let the loaf cool for 5 minutes.
6. Gently shake the bucket to remove the loaf.
7. Put to a cooling rack, slice, and serve.

Nutrition Information

- Calories: 140 Cal
- Fat: 2 g
- Carbohydrates:27 g
- Protein: 44 g
- Fibre: 2 g

MUSTARD FLAVOURED GENERAL BREAD

Servings: 2 loaves

Preparation time: **2 hours and 10 minutes**

Cook time: : **40 minutes**

Ingredients

- 1¼ cups milk
- Three tablespoons sunflower milk
- Three tablespoons sour cream
- Two tablespoons dry mustard
- One whole egg

Directions

1. Take out the bread maker's bucket and pour in milk and sunflower oil
   stir and then add sour cream and beaten egg.
2. Add flour, salt, sugar, mustard powder, vanilla sugar, and mix well.
3. Make a small groove in the flour and sprinkle the yeast.
4. Transfer the bucket to your bread maker and cover.
5. Set the program of your bread machine to Basic/White

- beaten
- ½ sachet sugar vanilla
- 4 cups flour
- One teaspoon dry yeast
- Two tablespoons sugar
- Two teaspoon salt

Bread and set crust type to Medium.

6. Press START.
7. Wait until the cycle completes.
8. Once the loaf is ready, take the bucket out and let it cool for 5 minutes.
9. Gently shake the bucket to remove the loaf.
10. Transfer to a cooling rack, slice, and serve.

Nutrition Information

- Calories: 340 Cal
- Fat: 10 g
- Carbohydrates:54 g
- Protein: 10 g
- Fibre: 1 g

COUNTRY WHITE BREAD

Servings: 2 loaves

Preparation time: **3 hours**

Cook time: : **45 minutes**

Ingredients

- Two teaspoons active dry yeast
- 1 1/2 tablespoon sugar
- 4 cups bread flour
- 1 1/2 teaspoon salt
- One large egg
- 1 1/2 tablespoon butter
- 1 cup warm milk,

Directions

1. Put all the liquid ingredients in the pan. Add all the dry ingredients except the yeast. Use your hand to form a hole in the middle of the dry ingredients. Put the yeast in the spot.

2. Secure the pan in the chamber and close the lid. Choose the basic setting and your preferred crust colour—press start.

3. Once done, transfer the baked bread to a wire rack. Slice once cooled.

with a temperature of
110 to 115 degrees F
(43 to 46 degrees C)

Nutrition Information

- Calories: 105 calories
- Total Carbohydrate: 0 g
- Total Fat: 0 g
- Protein: 0 g

OATMEAL BREAD

Servings: 2 loaves

Preparation time: 3 hours

Cook time: : 45 minutes

Ingredients

- Three teaspoons bread machine yeast
- Four teaspoons vital wheat gluten
- 4 cups bread flour
- One teaspoon salt
- 1 cup instant or regular oatmeal
- Two tablespoon maple syrup
- Two tablespoons

Directions

1. Put the pan's ingredients in this order: buttermilk, water, butter, maple syrup, oatmeal, salt, flour, gluten, and yeast.

2. Make Secure the pan in the machine, close the lid and turn it on.

3. Choose the basic setting and your preferred crust colour and press start.

4. Transfer the baked bread to a wire rack and allow to cool before slicing.

unsalted butter,
cubed

- 1/3 cup water, with a
temperature of 80 to
90 degrees F (26 to 32
degrees C)

- 1 1/2 cups
buttermilk, with a
temperature of 80 to
90 degrees F (26 to 32
degrees C)

Nutrition Information

- Calories: 269 calories
- Total Carbohydrate: 49 g
- Total Fat: 4 g
- Protein: 8 g

ANADAMA BREAD

Servings: 2 loaves

Preparation time: **3 hours**

Cook time: : **45 minutes**

Ingredients

- 1/2 cup sunflower seeds
- Two teaspoons bread machine yeast
- 4 1/2 cups bread flour
- 3/4 cup yellow cornmeal
- Two tablespoons unsalted butter, cubed
- 1 1/2 teaspoon salt

Directions

1. Put all the pan's ingredients, except the sunflower seeds, in this order: water, molasses, milk, salt, butter, cornmeal, flour, and yeast.

2. Put the pan in the machine and cover the lid.

3. Put the sunflower seeds in the fruit and nut dispenser.

4. Turn the machine on and choose the basic setting and your desired colour of the crust—press start.

- 1/4 cup dry skim milk powder
- 1/4 cup molasses
- 1 1/2 cups water, with a temperature of 80 to 90 degrees F (26 to 32 degrees C)

Nutrition Information

- Calories: 130 calories
- Total Carbohydrate: 25 g
- Total Fat: 2 g
- Protein: 3 g

APRICOT OAT

Servings: 1 loaf

Preparation time: 1 hour and 25 minutes

Cook time: : 25 minutes

Ingredients

- 4 1/4 cups bread flour
- 2/3 cup rolled oats
- One tablespoon white sugar
- Two teaspoons active dry yeast
- 1 1/2 teaspoons salt
- One teaspoon ground cinnamon
- Two tablespoons

Directions

1. Into the bread machine's pan, put the bread ingredients in the order suggested by the manufacturer. Then pout in dried apricots before the knead cycle completes.

2. Immediately remove bread from a machine when it's done and then glaze with warmed honey. Let to cool thoroughly before serving.

butter cut up

- 1 2/3 cups orange juice
- 1/2 cup diced dried apricots
- Two tablespoons honey, warmed

Nutrition Information

- Calories: 80 calories
- Total Carbohydrate: 14.4 g
- Cholesterol: 5 mg
- Total Fat: 2.3 g
- Protein: 1.3 g
- Sodium: 306 mg

BUTTERMILK WHITE BREAD

Servings: 1 loaf

Preparation time: 2 hours and 50 minutes

Cook time: : 25 minutes

Ingredients

- 1 1/8 cups water
- Three teaspoon honey
- One tablespoon margarine
- 1 1/2 teaspoon salt
- 3 cups bread flour
- Two teaspoons active dry yeast

Directions

1. Into the bread machine's pan, place the ingredients in the order suggested by the manufacturer: select medium crust and white bread settings. You can use a few yeasts during the hot and humid months of summer.

- Four teaspoons
  powdered buttermilk

Nutrition Information

- Calories: 34 calories
- Total Carbohydrate: 5.7 g
- Cholesterol: 1 mg
- Total Fat: 1 g
- Protein: 1 g
- Sodium: 313 mg

ENGLISH MUFFIN BREAD

Servings: 2 loaves

Preparation time: **2 hours and 30 minutes**

Cook time: : **15 minutes**

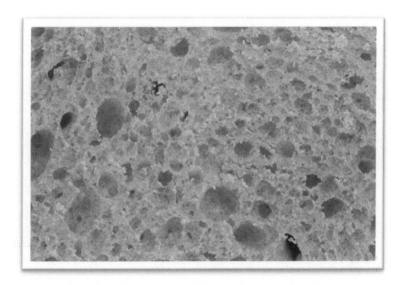

Ingredients

- 3 cups all-purpose flour
- 2 1/4 teaspoons active dry yeast
- 1/2 tablespoon white sugar
- One teaspoon salt
- 1/8 teaspoon baking powder
- 1 cup warm milk

Directions

1. Into the bread machine pan, put the ingredients according to the manufacturer's recommendations. Set the machine to the dough cycle.

2. Separate the dough into two unequal portions and then form into loaves. Put one leg in a 9 x 5-inch loaf pan and the other in a 7 x 3-inch loaf pan. It's recommended to use non-stick pans, although greased and floured standard pans will be enough. Need to cover the pans, then let the dough rise until it becomes doubled size.

3. Bake for about 15 minutes at 205 degrees C (400 degrees F). My grandmother usually bakes for longer to have a

- 1/4 cup water .... more browned and chewier crust.

Nutrition Information

- Calories: 64 calories
- Total Carbohydrate: 12.8 g
- Cholesterol: < 1 mg
- Total Fat: 0.4 g
- Protein: 2.1 g

HOMEMADE WONDERFUL BREAD

Servings: 2 loaves

Preparation time: 3 hours and 25 minutes

Cook time: : 15 minutes

Ingredients

- 2 1/2 teaspoons active dry yeast
- 1/4 cup warm water
- One tablespoon white sugar
- 4 cups all-purpose flour
- 1/4 cup dry potato flakes
- 1/4 cup dry milk

Directions

1. Prepare the yeast, 1/4 cup warm water and sugar to whisk and then let it sit in 15 minutes.

2. Take all ingredients together with yeast mixture to put in the pan of bread machine according to the manufacturer's recommended order. Choose basic and light crust settings.

- powder
- Two teaspoons salt
- 1/4 cup white sugar
- Two tablespoons margarine
- 1 cup of warm water(45 degrees C)

Nutrition Information

- Calories: 162 calories
- Total Carbohydrate: 31.6 g
- Cholesterol: < 1 mg
- Total Fat: 1.8 g
- Protein: 4.5 g

HONEY WHITE BREAD

Servings: 1 loaf

Preparation time: 3 hours and 25 minutes

Cook time: : 15 minutes

Ingredients

- 1 cup milk
- Three tablespoons unsalted butter, melted
- Two tablespoons honey
- 3 cups bread flour
- 3/4 teaspoon salt
- 3/4 teaspoon vitamin c powder

Directions

3. Follow the order as directed in your bread machine manual on how to assemble the ingredients. Use the setting for the Basic Bread cycle.

- 3/4 teaspoon ground ginger
- 1 1/2 teaspoons active dry yeast

Nutrition Information

- Calories: 172 Cal
- Carbohydrates: 28.9 g
- Cholesterol: 9 mg
- Fat: 3.9 g
- Protein: 5 g

Chapter 14: Pleasure Bread

CRISP WHITE BREAD

Servings: 1 loaf (10 slices)

Preparation time: **2 hour and 30 minutes**

Cook time: : **1 hour and 30 minutes**

Ingredients

- ¾ cup lukewarm water (80 degrees F)
- One tablespoon butter, melted
- One tablespoon white sugar
- ¾ teaspoon sea salt

Directions

4. Prepare all of the ingredients for your bread and measuring means (a cup, a spoon, kitchen scales).

5. Carefully measure the ingredients into the pan.

6. Put all the ingredients into a bread bucket in the right order, following the manual for your bread machine.

7. Close the cover. Select your bread machine program to BASIC / WHITE BREAD and choose the crust colour to

- Two tablespoons of milk powder
- 2 cups wheat flour
- ¾ teaspoon active dry yeast

MEDIUM.

8. Press START. Wait until the program completes.
9. When done, take the bucket out and let it cool for 5-10 minutes.
10. Shake the loaf from the pan and let cool for 30 minutes on a cooling rack.
11. Slice and serve.

Nutrition Information

- Calories 113
- Total Fat 1.4g
- Saturated Fat 0.8g
- Cholesterol 3g
- Sodium 158mg
- Total Carbohydrate 21.6g
- Dietary Fiber 0.7g
- Total Sugars 2.1g
- Protein 3.3g

MEDITERRANEAN SEMOLINA BREAD

Servings: 1 loaf (16 slices)

Preparation time: 2 hours

Cook time: : 30 minutes

Ingredients

- 1 cup lukewarm water (80 degrees F)
- One teaspoon salt
- 2½ tablespoons butter, melted
- 2½ teaspoons white sugar
- 2¼ cups all-purpose flour
- 1/3 cups semolina

Directions

1. Prepare all of the ingredients for your bread and measuring means (a cup, a spoon, kitchen scales).
2. Carefully measure the ingredients into the pan.
3. Put all the ingredients into a bread bucket in the right order. Follow your manual for the bread machine.
4. Close the cover.
5. Select your bread machine's program to ITALIAN BREAD / SANDWICH mode and choose the crust colour to MEDIUM.
6. Press START. Wait until the program completes.

- 1½ teaspoons active dry yeast

7. When done, take the bucket out and let it cool for 5-10 minutes.

8. Shake the loaf from the pan and let cool for 30 minutes on a cooling rack.

9. Slice and serve.

Nutrition Information

- Calories 243
- Total Fat 8.1g
- Saturated Fat 4.9g
- Cholesterol 20g
- Sodium 203mg
- Total Carbohydrate 37g
- Dietary Fiber 1.5g
- Total Sugars 2.8g
- Protein 5.3g

MUSTARD SOUR CREAM BREAD

Servings: 1 loaf

Preparation time: 1 hour

Cook time: : 1 hour

Ingredients

- 1¼ cups (320 ml) lukewarm milk
- Three tablespoons sunflower oil
- Three tablespoons

Directions

1. Prepare all of the ingredients for your bread and measuring means (a cup, a spoon, kitchen scales).
2. Carefully measure the ingredients into the pan.
3. Put all the ingredients into a bread bucket in the right order, follow your manual for the bread machine.

- sour cream
- Two tablespoons dry mustard
- One egg
- ½ sachet sugar vanilla
- 4 cups (690 g) wheat flour
- One teaspoon active dry yeast
- Two tablespoons white sugar
- Two teaspoons sea salt

4. Cover it. Select the program of your bread machine to BASIC and choose the crust colour to MEDIUM.

5. Press START. Wait until the program completes.

6. When done, take the bucket out and let it cool for 5-10 minutes.

7. Shake the loaf from the pan and let cool for 30 minutes on a cooling rack.

8. Slice, serve and enjoy the taste of fragrant homemade bread.

Nutrition Information

- Calories 340
- Total Fat 9.2g
- Saturated Fat 1.9g
- Cholesterol 26g
- Sodium 614mg

ITALIAN CIABATTA

Servings: 2 loaves

Preparation time: 30 minutes

Cook time: : 25 minutes

Ingredients

- 1 ½ cups water
- 1 ½ teaspoons salt
- 1 teaspoon white sugar
- 1 tablespoon olive oil
- 3 ¼ cups bread flour
- 1 ½ teaspoons bread machine yeast

Directions

1. Place the ingredients into the pan of the bread machine in the order suggested by the manufacturer. Select the Dough cycle, and Start. Carefully measure the ingredients into the pan.

2. When the cycle is completed, the dough will be a sticky and wet. Do not add more flour. Place the dough on a generously floured board, cover with a large bowl, and let it rest for 15 minutes.

3. Select your bread machine's program to ITALIAN BREAD / SANDWICH mode and choose the crust color to MEDIUM.

4. Lightly flour baking sheets or line them with parchment paper. Using a knife, divide the dough into 2 pieces, and form each into a 3x14-inch oval. Place the loaves on a sheet and dust it lightly with some flour. Cover it, and let it rise in a draft-free place for approximately 45 minutes.

5. Spritz the loaves with water. Place the loaves in the oven, positioned on the middle rack. Bake until golden brown, 25 to 30 minutes.

6. Serve and enjoy!

Nutrition Information

- Calories 73
- Total Fat 0.9g
- Cholesterol 0 mg
- Sodium 146.3 mg
- Total Carbohydrate 13.7g

OAT MOLASSES BREAD

Servings: 1 loaf

Preparation time: **2 hours**

Cook time: : **1 hour**

Ingredients

- 16 slice bread (2 pounds)
- 1 1/3 cups boiling water
- ¾ cup old-fashioned oats
- Three tablespoons butter
- One large egg lightly beaten

Directions

1. Add the boiling water and oats to a mixing bowl. Allow the oats to soak well and cool down completely. Do not drain the water.

2. Choose the size of bread you would like to make, then measure your ingredients.

3. Add the soaked oats, along with any remaining water, to the bread pan.

4. Put the remaining ingredients in the bread pan in the order listed above.

5. Place the pan in the bread machine, then cover.

- Two teaspoons table salt
- ¼ cup honey
- 1½ tablespoons dark molasses
- 4 cups white bread flour
- 2½ teaspoons bread machine yeast
- 12 slice bread (1½ pounds)
- 1 cup boiling water
- ½ cup old-fashioned oats
- Two tablespoons butter
- One large egg lightly beaten
- 1½ teaspoons table salt
- Three tablespoons honey
- One tablespoon dark molasses
- 3 cups white bread flour
- Two teaspoons bread machine yeast

6. Press on the machine. Select the Basic setting then the loaf size, and finally, the crust colour. Start the cycle.

7. When the process is finished, then when the bread is baked, remove the pan. Use a potholder as the handle. Rest for a while

8. Take out the bread from the pan and place it in a wire rack. Let it cool for at least 10 minutes before slicing.

Nutrition Information

- Calories 160, Fat 7.1 g
- carbs 18 g
- sodium 164 mg
- protein 5.1 g

WHOLE WHEAT CORN BREAD

Servings: 1 loaf

Preparation time: 2 hours

Cook time: : 1 hour

Ingredients

- 16 slice bread (2 pounds)
- 1 1/3 cups lukewarm water
- Two tablespoons light brown sugar
- One large egg beaten
- Two tablespoons unsalted butter, melted

Directions

1. Choose the size of loaf you would like to make and measure your ingredients.
2. Put the ingredients in a pan in the order list above.
3. Put the pan in the bread machine and cover it.
4. Switch on the bread maker. Select the Basic setting then the loaf size, and finally, the crust colour. Start the process.
5. When the process is finished, when the bread is baked, remove the pan from the machine. Use a potholder as the handle. Rest for a while.
6. Take out the bread from the pan and allow to cool on a

- 1½ teaspoons table salt
- ¾ cup whole wheat flour
- ¾ cup cornmeal
- 2¾ cups white bread flour
- 2½ teaspoons bread machine yeast
- 12 slice bread (1½ pounds)
- 1 cup lukewarm water
- 1½ tablespoons light brown sugar
- One medium egg beaten
- 1½ tablespoons unsalted butter, melted
- 1½ teaspoons table salt
- ½ cup whole wheat flour
- ½ cup cornmeal
- 2 cups of white bread flour
- 1½ teaspoons bread machine yeast

wire rack for at least 10 minutes before slicing.

Nutrition Information

- Calories 146, Fat 5.7 g
- carbs 19.3 g
- sodium 124 mg
- protein 4.8 g

WHEAT BRAN BREAD

Servings: 1 loaf

Preparation time: 2 hours

Cook time: : 1 hour

Ingredients

- 16 slice bread (2 pounds)
- 1½ cups lukewarm milk
- Three tablespoons unsalted butter, melted
- ¼ cup of sugar
- Two teaspoons table salt

Directions

1. Choose the size of loaf you would like to make and measure your ingredients.

2. Put the ingredients to the bread pan in the order listed above.

3. Put the pan in the bread machine and close the lid.

4. Switch on the bread maker. Select the Basic setting then the loaf size, and finally, the crust colour. Start the process.

5. When the process is finished, and the bread is baked, remove the pan from the machine. Use a potholder as the

- ½ cup wheat bran
- 3½ cups white bread flour
- Two teaspoons bread machine yeast
- 12 slice bread (1½ pounds)
- 1 1/8 cups lukewarm milk
- 2¼ tablespoons unsalted butter, melted
- Three tablespoons sugar
- 1½ teaspoons table salt
- 1/3 cup wheat bran
- 2 2/3 cups of white bread flour
- 1½ teaspoons bread machine yeast

handle. Rest for a few minutes.

6. Take out the bread from the pan and allow to cool on a wire rack for at least 10 minutes before slicing.

Nutrition Information

- Calories: 147 Cal
- Fat: 2.8 g
- Carbohydrates: 24.6 g
- Sodium: 312 mg

Chapter 15: International bread

GARLIC AND HERB FLATBREAD SOURDOUGH

Servings: 12 pcs

Preparation time: 1 hour

Cook time: : 20-30 minutes

Ingredients

- Dough
- 1 cup sourdough starter, fed or unfed
- 3/4 cup warm water

Directions

1. Combine all the dough ingredients in the bowl of a stand mixer, and knead until smooth. Place in a lightly greased bowl and let rise for at least one hour. Punch down, then let rise again for at least one hour.

2. To prepare the topping

- Two teaspoons instant yeast
- 3 cups all-purpose flour
- 1 1/2 teaspoons salt
- Three tablespoons olive oil
- Topping
- 1/2 teaspoon dried thyme
- 1/2 teaspoon dried oregano
- 1/2 teaspoon dried marjoram
- One teaspoon garlic powder
- 1/4 teaspoon onion powder
- 1/4 teaspoon salt
- 1/4 teaspoon pepper
- Three tablespoons olive oil

mix all ingredients except the olive oil in a small bowl.

3. Lightly grease a 9x13 baking pan or standard baking sheet, and pat and roll the dough into a long rectangle in the pan. Brush the olive oil over the dough, and sprinkle the herb and seasoning mixture over the top. Cover and let rise for 15-20 minutes.

4. Preheat oven to 425F and bake for 25-30 minutes.

Nutrition Information

- Calories: 89 Cal
- Fat: 3.7 g
- Protein: 1.8 g

GARLIC BREAD

Servings: one loaf (15 slices)

Preparation time: **5 minutes**

Cook time: : **3 hours**

Ingredients

- 1 ⅜ cups water
- 3 tablespoons olive oil
- 1 teaspoon minced garlic
- 4 cups bread flour
- 3 tablespoons white sugar
- 2 teaspoons salt
- ¼ cup grated

Directions

5. Place ingredients in the bread machine pan in the order suggested by the manufacturer.
6. Select Basic or White Bread cycle, and press Start.

Parmesan cheese

- 1 teaspoon dried basil
- 1 teaspoon garlic powder
- 3 tablespoons chopped fresh chives
- 1 teaspoon coarsely ground black pepper
- 2 ½ teaspoons bread machine yeast

Nutrition Information

- Calories: 175 Cal
- Fat: 3.7 g
- Carbohydrates: 29.7 g
- Sodium: 332.4mg

SOURDOUGH BOULE

Ingredients

- 275g Warm Water
- 500g sourdough starter
- 550g all-purpose flour
- 20g Salt

Directions

1. Combine the flour, warm water, starter, and let sit, covered for at least 30 minutes.

2. After letting it sit, stir in the salt, and turn the dough out onto a floured surface. It will be quite sticky, but that's okay. Flatten the dough slightly (it's best to "slap" it onto the counter), then fold it in half a few times.

3. Cover the dough and let it rise. Repeat the slap and fold a few more times. Now cover the dough and let it rise for 2-4 hours.

4. When the dough at least doubles in size, gently pull it, so

the top of the dough is taught. Repeat several times. Let it rise for 2-4 hours once more.

5. Preheat to oven to 475F, and either place a baking stone or a cast iron pan in the oven to preheat. Place the risen dough on the rock or pot, and score the top in several spots. Bake for 20 minutes, then lower the heat to 425F and bake for 25-35 minutes more. The boule will be golden brown.

Nutrition Information

- Calories: 243 Cal
- Fat: 0.7 g
- Protein: 6.9 g

HERBED BAGUETTE

Servings: one loaf (12 slices)

Preparation time: 45 minutes

Cook time: : 20-25 minutes

Ingredients

- 1 1/4 cups warm water
- 2 cups sourdough starter, either fed or unfed
- 4 to 5 cups all-purpose flour
- 2 1/2 teaspoons salt
- Two teaspoons sugar
- One tablespoon

Directions

1. In the bowl of a stand mixer, combine all ingredients, knead with a dough hook (or use your hands) until smooth dough forms -- about 7 to 10 minutes, if needed, add more flour.

2. Place the dough in an oiled bowl, cover, and allow to rise for about 2 hours.

3. Punch down the dough, and divide it into three pieces. Shape each piece of dough into a baguette -- about 16 inches long. You can do this by rolling the dough into a log
folding it, rolling it into a log

instant yeast

- One tablespoon fresh oregano, chopped
- One teaspoon fresh rosemary, chopped
- One tablespoon fresh basil, chopped
- any other desired herbs

then folding it and moving it again.

4. Place the rolled baguette dough onto lined baking sheets, and cover. Let rise for one hour.

5. Preheat oven to 425F, and bake for 20-25 minutes

Nutrition Information

- Calories: 197 Cal
- Fat: 0.6 g
- Protein: 5.8 g

PUMPERNICKEL BREAD

Servings: one loaf (12 slices)

Preparation time: 2 hours and 10 minutes

Cook time: : 50 minutes

Ingredients

- 1 1/8 cups warm water
- 1 ½ tablespoon vegetable oil
- 1/3 cup molasses
- Three tablespoons cocoa
- One tablespoon caraway seed

Directions

1. Add all ingredients to the bread machine pan.
2. Choose the basic bread cycle.
3. Take the bread out to cool and enjoy!

(optional)

- 1 ½ teaspoon salt
- 1 ½ cups of bread flour
- 1 cup of rye flour
- 1 cup whole wheat flour
- 1 ½ tablespoon of vital wheat gluten (optional)
- 2 ½ teaspoon of bread machine yeast

Nutrition Information

- Calories: 97 Cal
- Fat: 1 g
- Carbohydrates:19 g
- Protein: 3 g

SAUERKRAUT RYE

Servings: one loaf

Preparation time: 2 hours and 20 minutes

Cook time: : 50 minutes

Ingredients

- 1 cup sauerkraut, rinsed and drained
- 3/4 cup of warm

Directions

1. Add all of the ingredients to your bread machine.
2. Set the program of your bread machine to Basic/White Bread and set crust type to Medium

- water
- 1½ tablespoons molasses
- 1½ tablespoons butter
- 1½ tablespoons brown sugar
- One teaspoon caraway seeds
- 1½ teaspoons salt
- 1 cup rye flour
- 2 cups bread flour
- 1½ teaspoons active dry yeast

3. Press START
4. Wait until the cycle completes
5. Once the loaf is ready, take the bucket out and let the loaf cool for 5 minutes
6. Gently shake the bucket to remove the loaf
7. Transfer to a cooling rack, slice and serve

Nutrition Information

- Calories: 74 Cal
- Fat: 2 g
- Carbohydrates: 12 g
- Protein: 2 g
- Fiber: 1 g

CRUSTY SOURDOUGH BREAD

Servings: one loaf

Preparation time: 15 minutes

Cook time: : 50 minutes

Ingredients

- 1/2 cup water
- 3 cups bread flour
- Two tablespoons sugar
- 1 ½ teaspoon salt
- One teaspoon bread machine or quick active dry yeast

Directions

1. Measure 1 cup of starter and remaining bread ingredients, add to bread machine pan.
2. Choose the basic/white bread cycle with medium or light crust colour.

Nutrition Information

- Calories: 165 calories
- Total Carbohydrate: 37 g
- Total Fat: 0 g
- Protein: 5 g
- Sodium: 300 mg
- Fiber: 1 g

HONEY SOURDOUGH BREAD

Servings: one loaf

Preparation time: 15 minutes

Cook time: : 3 hours

Ingredients

- 2/3 cup sourdough starter
- 1/2 cup water
- One tablespoon vegetable oil
- Two tablespoons honey
- 1/2 teaspoon salt
- 1/2 cup high protein wheat flour

Directions

1. Measure 1 cup of starter and remaining bread ingredients, add to bread machine pan.

2. Choose the basic/white bread cycle with medium or light crust colour.

- 2 cups bread flour
- One teaspoon active dry yeast

Nutrition Information

- Calories: 175 calories
- Total Carbohydrate: 33 g
- Total Fat: 0.3 g
- Protein: 5.6 g
- Sodium: 121 mg
- Fiber: 1.9 g

MULTIGRAIN SOURDOUGH BREAD

Servings: one loaf

Preparation time: 15 minutes

Cook time: : 3 hours

Ingredients

- 2 cups sourdough starter
- Two tablespoons butter or two tablespoons olive oil
- 1/2 cup milk
- One teaspoon salt
- 1/4 cup honey
- 1/2 cup sunflower seeds

Directions

1. Add ingredients to the bread machine pan.
2. Choose the dough cycle.
3. Conventional Oven:
4. When the cycle is complete, remove dough and place on a lightly floured surface and shape into a loaf.
5. Place in a greased loaf pan, cover, and rise until bread is a couple of inches above the edge.
6. Bake at 375 degrees for 40 to 50 minutes.

- 1/2 cup millet or 1/2 cup amaranth or 1/2 cup quinoa
- 3 1/2 cups multi-grain flour

Nutrition Information

- Calories: 110 calories
- Total Carbohydrate: 13.5 g
- Total Fat: 1.8 g
- Protein: 2.7 g
- Sodium: 213 mg
- Fiber: 1.4 g

OLIVE AND GARLIC SOURDOUGH BREAD

Servings: one loaf

Preparation time: 15 minutes

Cook time: : 3 hours

Ingredients

- 2 cups sourdough starter
- Two tablespoons butter or two tablespoons olive oil
- 1/2 cup milk
- One teaspoon salt
- 1/4 cup honey
- 1/2 cup sunflower seeds

Directions

1. Add ingredients to the bread machine pan.
2. Choose the dough cycle.
3. Conventional Oven:
4. When the cycle is complete, remove dough and place on a lightly floured surface and shape into a loaf.
5. Place in a greased loaf pan, cover, and rise until bread is a couple of inches above the edge.
6. Bake at 375 degrees for 40 to 50 minutes.

- 1/2 cup millet or 1/2 cup amaranth or 1/2 cup quinoa
- 3 1/2 cups multi-grain flour

Nutrition Information

- Calories: 110 calories
- Total Carbohydrate: 13.5 g
- Total Fat: 1.8 g
- Protein: 2.7 g
- Sodium: 213 mg
- Fiber: 1.4 g

CZECH SOURDOUGH BREAD

Servings: one loaf

Preparation time: **15 minutes**

Cook time: : **3 hours**

Ingredients

- 1 cup non-dairy milk
- One tablespoon salt
- One tablespoon honey
- 1 cup sourdough starter
- 1 1/2 cups rye flour
- 1 cup bread flour

Directions

1. Add ingredients to the bread machine pan.
2. Choose the dough cycle.
3. The dough will need to rise, up to 24 hours, in the bread machine until doubles in size.
4. After rising
   bake in the bread machine for one hour.

- 3⁄4 cup wheat flour
- 1⁄2 cup grated half-baked potato
- Five tablespoons wheat gluten
- Two teaspoons caraway seeds

Nutrition Information

- Calories: 198 calories
- Total Carbohydrate: 39.9 g
- Total Fat: 0.8 g
- Protein: 6.5 g
- Sodium: 888 mg
- Fiber: 4.3 g

FRENCH SOURDOUGH BREAD

Servings: 2 loaves

Preparation time: **15 minutes**

Cook time: : **3 hours**

Ingredients

- 2 cups sourdough starter
- One teaspoon salt
- 1/2 cup water

Directions

1. Add ingredients to the bread machine pan, saving cornmeal for later.
2. Choose the dough cycle.
3. Conventional Oven:

- 4 cups white bread flour
- Two tablespoons white cornmeal

4. Preheat oven to 375 degrees.
5. At the end of the dough cycle, turn the dough out onto a floured surface.
6. Add flour if the dough is sticky.
7. Divide dough into two portions and flatten into an oval shape 1 ½ inch thick.
8. Fold ovals in half lengthwise and pinch seams to elongate.
9. Sprinkle cornmeal onto the baking sheet and place the loaves seam side down.
10. Cover and let rise in until about doubled.
11. Place a shallow pan of hot water on the lower shelf of the oven
12. Use a knife to make shallow, diagonal slashes in tops of loaves
13. Place the loaves in the oven and spray with a fine water mister. Spray the oven walls as well.
14. Repeat spraying three times at one-minute intervals.
15. Remove pan of water after 15 minutes of baking
16. Thoroughly bake for 30 to 40 minutes or until golden brown.

Nutrition Information

- Calories: 937 calories
- Total Carbohydrate: 196 g
- Total Fat: 0.4 g
- Protein: 26.5 g
- Sodium: 1172 mg
- Fiber: 7.3 g